The Wee
Book of

IRISh
wit
&
malarkey

The Wee Book of
IRISH wit & malarkey

**A Rake of Clever Craic and Wisdom
for Jackeens, Culchies, and Eejits**

Sean McCann and Paul Ryan

METRO BOOKS
NEW YORK

contents

introduction

finding the wit in ireland

the greatest wit in Ireland is 'yer man'. He is also the finest humorist as well as being the leading authority on everything that grows, breeds, breathes, walks, thinks, or computes in the land. No one doubts the authenticity of the word of 'yer man'. He is Yeats, De Valera, Wilde, Behan, *Dublin Opinion*, and Paddy the Irishman rolled into one. He is the greatest asset to a land that is notorious for its tender toes because he has the magnificent advantage of never being held responsible for anything he says or does.

Among the Irish 'yer man' is the maker of laughs, the man O'Casey had in mind when he said that the Irish thinking is as sober as the English except that it is always 'given the halo of a laugh'. 'Yer man' is the halo-maker. Side by side with him are men whose witticisms have stuck and will forever be linked with their names. These—plus 'yer man'—present a happily malicious collection, immense enough to scarify anyone who looks deeply at Irish wit.

For century after century the Irish have mixed wit with wisdom, porter with whiskey, all to practically the same intoxicating effect although still retaining a clarity that allows them to tell the truth about life and people. And nothing is funnier than the truth—

when you hear it between drinks. For a brief sentence or two, read the list a compiler has to contend with: AE, Barrington, Behan, Father Healy, Kettle, Joyce, Moore, O'Casey, O'Connell, Roche, Swift, Shaw, Stephens, Wilde, Yeats…and just to complete the A to Z there was Zozimus. But never mind, that's enough names for now.

The width of wit has an obesity that would defy any slimming diet. There is everything from the traditional Bull to the scorpion sting, from soft blatherings to verbal karate.

Dean Jonathan Swift could be most un-Christian with his cruel and often repellent wit, once even suggesting that a cure for famine was to fatten surplus babies for food. Scorpion-like was Susan Mitchell's suggestion that the reason a Catholic wife could not be buried in her Protestant husband's grave was that 'it might mar the perfection of a Protestant resurrection.'

Oscar Wilde is in his own category with the amount of wit and wisdom that came from his pen and mouth. You will notice a plethora of his quotes in this volume, as the man had something witty to

say about practically everything. He left a legacy that is unlikely ever to be forgotten; a legacy of plays, poetry, criticism—but none more so than his ability as a wit.

The wit of 'yer man' is generally the good-humoured kind; saying serious things in a way that seem funny when you see how serious they are. An English tourist asked 'yer man' what the road from Ballina to Belmullet was like because he had heard it was very rough. 'Well, sir,' he said after a few seconds contemplation, 'it's the sort of road I wouldn't like to have to praise.' And again the soft wit carried off an awkward situation when 'yer man' was asked to recommend one of the two hotels in a southern town. 'Well, it's like this,' he said, 'whichever one ye stay at ye'll wish it had been the other.'

This is the softness that takes the edge off the epithets and sarcasm that seldom give a man a chance to reply. Certainly there has been enough of them all in Ireland through the years. James Stephens said that during his time—the early 1900s—Dublin functioned in a state of verbal excitement for everyone was using prose instead of grammar.

On the other hand there is the Bull—a supposedly Irish form of unconscious humour—one man defined it as the saying that contradicts itself, in a manner palpably absurd to listeners but unperceived by the person who makes it. Less word-locked was the definition the late Richard Hayeard gave to me:

I look across the hedge—twelve cows I see,
The night is clear, the moon is at the full,

The twelve are laying silent round a tree
And one is standing; one—an Irish Bull.

But the most famous definition, attributed to Professor Mahaffy, was that an 'Irish Bull is always pregnant'. A definition that has a lot of truth in it, if you see what I mean.

It is often the way things are said that makes Irish wit, and makes it so embracing. There is no restriction on subject matter. In England the new arrival is warned not to get into any arguments or to make jokes about religion or politics. In Ireland it is the very opposite. No good conversation would be complete without one—or both—of them. And where's the man who would omit the other Irish 'topics'? An English judge, recently reducing an

Irishman's sentence for house breaking and larceny from five years to three, justified his decision by saying: 'Most of his previous convictions were for ordinary Irish offences: drunk and disorderly and assaulting the police.' But, of course, Irish offences in England are very different from Irish offences in Ireland. Change the phraseology from 'drunk and disorderly and assaulting the police' to 'a drop of the hard stuff, a bit of devilment, and a logical argument' and the whole affair assumes different proportions.

Anyway, whatever your views about the Irish, their Bulls or their malapropisms, their howlers or their distortions, you just cannot get away from the fact that from the mythical Cuchulainn to the far from mythical Behan they have left a treasury of wit. Any collection must, of course, be a very personal affair, which will mean that there will always be the fellow who will say: 'Sure he left the best ones out... come here till I tell you...' And to prove his point he will whisper his own collection that, with Dublin's fine acoustics, will send everyone home asking: 'Did you hear "yer man"?'

—Sean McCann

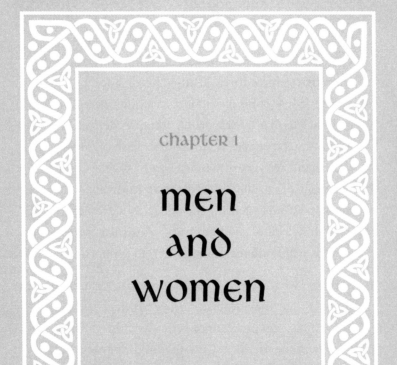

chapter 1

men
and
women

Men become old, but they never become good.

—Oscar Wilde, *Lady Windermere's Fan*

♣

Most people are other people. Their thoughts are someone else's opinions, their lives a mimicry, their passions a quotation.

—Oscar Wilde

♣

If a woman really repents, she never wishes to return to the society that has made or seen her ruin.

—Oscar Wilde, *Lady Windermere's Fan*

♣

By persistently remaining single, a man converts himself into a permanent public temptation.

—Oscar Wilde

♣

 She who hesitates is won.

—Oscar Wilde

Donegal girls have the permission of the Pope to wear the thick end of their legs below the knee.

—Anonymous

A man who can dominate a London dinner-table can dominate the world. The future belongs to the dandy. It is the exquisites who are going to rule.

—Oscar Wilde, *A Woman of No Importance*

A man who can dominate a London dinner-table can dominate the world. The future belongs to the dandy. It is the exquisites who are going to rule.

No man is rich enough to buy back his past.

—Oscar Wilde, *An Ideal Husband*

Wicked women bother one. Good women bore one. That is the only difference between them.

—Oscar Wilde, *Lady Windermere's Fan*

I prefer women with a past. They're always so damned amusing to talk to.

—Oscar Wilde, *Lady Windermere's Fan*

OVERHEARD IN DUBLIN

"I'd love to be a man, Maisie, then I wouldn't have to kiss someone who had'nt washed or shaved for three days."

When a man is old enough to do wrong he should be old enough to do right also.

—Oscar Wilde, *A Woman of No Importance*

🍀

Mrs. Allonby: The Ideal Man...he should always say much more than he means, and always mean much more than he says.

—Oscar Wilde, *A Woman of No Importance*

Man is least himself when he talks in his own person. Give him a mask, and he will tell you the truth.

—Oscar Wilde, "The Critic as Artist"

Good looks are a snare that every sensible man would like to be caught in.

—Oscar Wilde, *The Importance of Being Earnest*

A wonderful race is the race of women; they're misunderstood by men, for they understand only lovers, children and flowers.

—George Moore

🍀

The mind of a thoroughly well-informed man is a dreadful thing. It is like a bric-a-brac shop, all monsters and dust, with everything priced above its proper value.

—Oscar Wilde, *The Picture of Dorian Gray*

The true perfection of man lies, not in what man has, but in what man is.

—Oscar Wilde

What is a cynic?
A man who knows the
price of everything and
the value of nothing.

—Oscar Wilde, *Lady Windemere's Fan*

Men of thought should have nothing to do with action.

—Oscar Wilde, *Vera, or The Nihilists*

One is tempted to define man as a rational animal who always loses his temper when he is called upon to act in accordance with the dictates of reason.

—Oscar Wilde, "The Critic as Artist"

A gentleman is one who never hurts anyone's feelings unintentionally.

—Oscar Wilde

♣

Mrs. Allonby: I delight in men over seventy; they always offer one the devotion of a lifetime.

—Oscar Wilde, *A Woman of No Importance*

♣

The evolution of man is slow. The injustice of man is great.

—Oscar Wilde, "The Soul of Man Under Socialism"

I sometimes think that God, in creating man, somewhat overestimated His ability.

—Oscar Wilde

Women—Sphinxes without secrets.

—Oscar Wilde, *A Woman of No Importance*

🍀

Bachelor: A man who shirks responsibility and duties.

—George Bernard Shaw

🍀

A man who moralises is usually a hypocrite, and
a woman who moralises is invariably plain.

—Oscar Wilde, *Lady Windermere's Fan*

🍀

She is a peacock in everything but beauty.

—Oscar Wilde, *The Picture of Dorian Gray*

🍀

As long as a woman can look ten years younger
than her own daughter, she is perfectly satisfied.

—Oscar Wilde, *The Picture of Dorian Gray*

To be perfectly proportioned is a rare thing in an age when so many women are either over life-size or insignificant.

—Oscar Wilde, "Lord Arthur Savile's Crime"

Woman begins by resisting a man's advances and ends by blocking his retreat.

—Oscar Wilde

Lady Windermere: I don't like compliments, and I don't see why a man should think he is pleasing a woman enormously when he says to her a whole heap of things that he doesn't mean.

—Oscar Wilde, *Lady Windermere's Fan*

She wore far too much rouge last night and not quite enough clothes. That is always a sign of despair in a woman.

—Oscar Wilde, *An Ideal Husband*

One should never give a woman anything she can't wear in the evening.

—Oscar Wilde, *An Ideal Husband*

♣

When she is in a very smart gown, she looks like an edition de luxe of a wicked French novel meant specially for the English market.

—Oscar Wilde, *The Importance of Being Earnest*

Women are meant to be loved, not to be understood.

—Oscar Wilde, "The Sphinx Without a Secret"

Miss Prism: A misanthrope I can understand— a woman-thrope, never!

—Oscar Wilde, *The Importance of Being Earnest*

She looks like a woman with a past. Most pretty women do.

—Oscar Wilde, *An Ideal Husband*

Woman: What is the difference between a man and a woman?
J.P. Mahaffy: I cannot conceive.

A woman will flirt with anybody in the world as long as other people are looking on.

—Oscar Wilde, *The Picture of Dorian Gray*

Thirty-five is a very attractive age; London society is full of women of the highest birth who have, of their own free choice, remained thirty-five for years.

—Oscar Wilde, *The Importance of Being Earnest*

What have women who have not sinned to do
with me, or I with them? We do not understand
each other.

—Oscar Wilde, *A Woman of No Importance*

Women, as some witty Frenchman once put it,
inspire us with the desire to do masterpieces, and
always prevent us from carrying them out.

—Oscar Wilde, *The Picture of Dorian Gray*

If a woman can't make her mistakes charming, she is only a female.

—Oscar Wilde, "Lord Arthur Savile's Crime"

No man has any real success in this world unless he has got women to back him, and women rule society.

—Oscar Wilde

A woman with a past has no future.

—Oscar Wilde

♣

Average Woman: One who is always a wish ahead of her budget.

—*Irish Echo*

Women are a decorative sex. They never have anything to say, but they say it charmingly. Women represent the triumph of matter over mind, just as men represent the triumph of mind over morals.

—Oscar Wilde, *The Picture of Dorian Gray*

Women have a much better time than men in this world; there are far more things forbidden to them.

—Oscar Wilde

I don't believe in women thinking too much. Women should think in moderation, as they should do all things in moderation.

—Oscar Wilde, *A Woman of No Importance*

Every woman is a rebel, and usually in wild revolt against herself.

—Oscar Wilde, *A Woman of No Importance*

The private lives of men and women should not be told to the public. The public have nothing to do with them at all.

—Oscar Wilde, "The Soul of Man Under Socialism"

It takes a thoroughly good woman to do a thoroughly stupid thing.

—Oscar Wilde, *Lady Windermere's Fan*

Between men and women there is no friendship possible. There is passion, enmity, worship, love, but no friendship.

—Oscar Wilde, *Lady Windermere's Fan*

A woman's life revolves in curves of emotion. It is upon lines of intellect that a man's life progresses.

—Oscar Wilde, *An Ideal Husband*

Women are never disarmed by compliments. Men always are. That is the difference between the sexes.

—Oscar Wilde, *An Ideal Husband*

All reformers are bachelors.

—George Moore

Talk to every woman as if you loved her, and to every man as if he bored you.

—Oscar Wilde

A bad man is the sort of man who admires innocence, and a bad woman is the sort of woman a man never gets tired of.

—Oscar Wilde, *A Woman of No Importance*

I am afraid that women appreciate cruelty, down-right cruelty, more than anything else. They have wonderfully primitive instincts. We have emancipated them, but they remain slaves looking for their masters all the same.

—Oscar Wilde, *The Picture of Dorian Gray*

♣

Women are not meant to judge us, but to forgive us when we need forgiveness. Pardon, not punishment, is their mission.

—Oscar Wilde, *An Ideal Husband*

I like men who have a future and women who have a past.

—Oscar Wilde, *The Picture of Dorian Gray*

No woman should ever be quite accurate about her age—it looks so calculating.

—Oscar Wilde

♣

All women become like their mothers. That is their tragedy. No man does. That's his.

—Oscar Wilde, *The Importance of Being Earnest*

♣

The history of women is the history of the worst form of tyranny the world has ever known. The tyranny of the weak over the strong. It is the only tyranny that lasts.

—Oscar Wilde, *A Woman of No Importance*

♣

How hard good women are! How weak bad men are!

—Oscar Wilde, *Lady Windermere's Fan*

Women's styles may change but their designs
remain the same.

—Oscar Wilde

Women treat us just as
humanity treats its gods.
They worship us and are
always bothering us to
do something for them.

—Oscar Wilde

A pessimist: A woman driver who's afraid she
won't be able to squeeze her car into a very small
parking space. An optimist is a man who believes
she won't try.

—Anonymous

A mask tells us more than a face.

—Oscar Wilde, "Pen, Pencil and Poison"

♣

With an evening coat and a white tie, anybody, even a stockbroker, can gain a reputation for being civilised.

—Oscar Wilde

♣

Crying is the refuge of plain women but the ruin of pretty ones.

—Oscar Wilde

chapter 2

friends
and
enemies

I have never given adoration to anyone except myself.

—Oscar Wilde

Good manners is the art of making those people easy with whom we converse. Whoever makes the fewest people uneasy, is the best bred in the company.

—Dean Jonathan Swift

On an individual who took himself too seriously:
[He is] afraid to smile lest anyone might suppose that he was too familiar with himself.

—John Philpot Curran

In a Dublin drawingroom a great number of mediocrities were airing their importance. One of those present informed John Philpot Curran that there was not a man amongst them who had not had a distinguished ancestor. Curran replied:
Bless my soul, what a crowd of anti-climaxes!

OVERHEARD IN DUBLIN

"That wan is yapping on an' on all bleedin' morning. Jaysus, whoever turned her on must have gone away and forgotten to come back and turn her off."

On hearing a passerby say, 'There goes that bloody fool Oscar Wilde,' Wilde remarked to his companion:
It's extraordinary how soon one gets known in London.

🍀

There is only one thing in the world worse than being talked about, and that is not being talked about.

—Oscar Wilde, *The Picture of Dorian Gray*

🍀

On an unnamed person:
He hasn't a single redeeming vice.

—Oscar Wilde

Formerly we used to canonise our heroes. The modern method is to vulgarise them. Cheap editions of great books may be delightful, but cheap editions of great men are absolutely detestable.

—Oscar Wilde, "The Critic as Artist"

I shall never make a new friend in my life, though perhaps a few after I die.

—Oscar Wilde

I must decline your invitation due to a subsequent engagement.

—Oscar Wilde

After a good dinner one can forgive anybody, even one's own relations.

—Oscar Wilde, *A Woman of No Importance*

I love scandals about other people, but scandals about myself don't interest me. They have not got the charm of novelty.

—Oscar Wilde, *The Picture of Dorian Gray*

I like persons better than principles and I like persons with no principles better than anything else in the world.

—Oscar Wilde, *The Picture of Dorian Gray*

Friends: Thermometers by which we may judge the temperature of our fortune.

—Countess of Blessington

I choose my friends for their good looks, my acquaintances for their good characters, and my enemies for their good intellects. A man cannot be too careful in the choice of his enemies.

—Oscar Wilde

Relations are simply a tedious pack of people, who haven't got the remotest knowledge of how to live, nor the smallest instinct about when to die.

—Oscar Wilde, *The Importance of Being Earnest*

overheard in dublin

WOMAN #1: Wouldn't ye think she'd take off some of the oul' cardigans now on a lovely fine day like this.

WOMAN #2: Jaysus, luv, them jumpers is part of her body at this stage, sure if she took any of them off now wouldn't her rib cage collapse?

I can't help detesting my relations. I suppose it comes from the fact that none of us stand other people having the same faults as ourselves.

—Oscar Wilde, *The Picture of Dorian Gray*

Every effect that one produces gives one an enemy.
To be popular one must be a mediocrity.

—Oscar Wilde, *The Picture of Dorian Gray*

♣

One can always be kind to people about whom one
cares nothing.

—Oscar Wilde, *The Picture of Dorian Gray*

OVERHEARD IN DUBLIN

WOMAN #1: Katie is great fun to talk to, she can't
say anything nice about anyone.
WOMAN #2: Yea, she's not prejudiced, she just hates
everybody.

I dare say that if I knew him I should not be his
friend at all. It is a very dangerous thing to know
one's friends.

—Oscar Wilde, "The Remarkable Rocket"

I think that generosity is the essence of friendship.

—Oscar Wilde, "The Devoted Friend"

♣

No one cares about distant relations nowadays.
They went out of fashion years ago.

—Oscar Wilde, "Lord Arthur Savile's Crime"

It is absurd to divide people into good and bad. People are either charming or tedious.

—Oscar Wilde, *Lady Windermere's Fan*

On a Limerick banker who was renowned for his
sagacity and had an iron leg:
His leg is the softest thing about him.

—John Philpot Curran

I always like to know everything about my new friends, and nothing about my old ones.

—Oscar Wilde, *The Picture of Dorian Gray*

What is the good of friendship if one cannot say exactly what one means?

—Oscar Wilde, "The Devoted Friend"

Tolerance: The suspicion that the other fellow might be right.

—Traditional

One has a right to judge a man by the effect he has over his friends.

—Oscar Wilde, *The Picture of Dorian Gray*

overheard in dublin

WOMAN #1: The bitch still isn't speaking to you? But I thought you'd made yer mind up not to talk to her.

WOMAN #2: Yea, but she didn't speak to me to give me a chance not to talk to her.

He would stab his best friend for the sake of writing an epigram on his tombstone.

—Oscar Wilde, *Vera, or The Nihilists*

I'm sure I don't know half the people who come to my house. Indeed, from all I hear, I shouldn't like to.

—Oscar Wilde, *An Ideal Husband*

Do not tell your troubles to one who has no pity.

—Traditional

overheard in Dublin

" Ah it's only poor Annie talking to herself again. The poor soul, she must get terrible stupid answers."

As a wicked man I am a complete failure. Why, there are lots of people who say I have never really done anything wrong in the whole course of my life. Of course, they only say it behind my back.

—Oscar Wilde, *Lady Windermere's Fan*

I have never, on my travels, ever met anything worse than myself.

—Brendan Behan

An acquaintance that begins with a compliment is sure to develop into a real friendship. It starts in the right manner.

—Oscar Wilde, *An Ideal Husband*

Laughter is not at all a bad beginning for a friendship, and it is far the best ending for one.

—Oscar Wilde, *The Picture of Dorian Gray*

It is perfectly monstrous the way people go about nowadays saying things against one behind one's back that are absolutely and entirely true.

—Oscar Wilde, *The Picture of Dorian Gray*

When one pays a visit it is for the purpose of wasting other people's time, not one's own.

—Oscar Wilde, *An Ideal Husband*

OVERHEARD IN DUBLIN

" He's like a blister, luv, he always appears after the work is done."

chapter 3

youth
and
aging

You've got to do your own growing no matter how tall your grandfather was.

—Traditional

The young are always ready to give those who are older than themselves the full benefit of their inexperience.

—Oscar Wilde

Little children who could neither walk nor talk were running around the streets cursing their Maker.

—Sir Boyle Roche

If you want to reach the age of eighty-five, get a stomach ulcer when you're twenty-five, and you'll take such good care of yourself, for fear of upsetting the ulcer, that you'll outlast all around you.

—Lynn Doyle

overheard in dublin

"That wan is as deaf as a door. The doctor examined her and told her that she had an insufficient passage and that if she heard anything it'd be a miracle. Well, she was as white as a maggot. She thought he said that she had a fish in her passage and that if she had anything it would be a mackerel, now I ask ye."

The secret of remaining young is never to have an emotion that is unbecoming.

—Oscar Wilde, *The Picture of Dorian Gray*

Youth isn't an affectation. Youth is an art.

—Oscar Wilde, *An Ideal Husband*

An inordinate passion for pleasure is the secret of remaining young.

—Oscar Wilde, "Lord Arthur Savile's Crime"

The pleasure to me was being with those who are young, bright, happy, careless and free. I do not like the sensible and I do not like the old.

—Oscar Wilde

A lot of modern upbringing consists of giving children their head and leaving them to find their feet.

—*Dublin Opinion*

The soul is born old but grows young. That is the comedy of life. And the body is born young and grows old. That is life's tragedy.

—Oscar Wilde, *A Woman of No Importance*

Observation is an old man's memory.

—Dean Jonathan Swift

n ot to marry a young woman.

Not to keep young company, unless they really desire it.

Not to be peevish, or morose, or suspicious.

Not to be fond of children or let them come near me hardly.

Not to boast of my former beauty or strength or favour with ladies.

Not to harken to flatteries, nor conceive I can be beloved by a young woman.

Not to set up for observing all these Rules for fear I should observe none.

— Dean Jonathan Swift, "When I Come to Be Old"

To get back one's youth, one has merely to repeat one's follies.

—Oscar Wilde

One should never make one's debut with a scandal. One should reserve that to give an interest to one's old age.

—Oscar Wilde, *The Picture of Dorian Gray*

Youth is the one thing worth having.

—Oscar Wilde, *The Picture of Dorian Gray*

🍀

Nothing ages like happiness.

—Oscar Wilde, *An Ideal Husband*

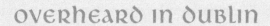

OVERHEARD IN DUBLIN

WOMAN: What are you goin' to be when you grow up, son?
BOY: Bigger, missus.
WOMAN: And were ye born in Dublin, son?
BOY: Yea.
WOMAN: What part?
BOY: All of me.

The condition of perfection is idleness; the aim of perfection is youth.

—Oscar Wilde, "Phrases and Philosophies
for the Use of the Young"

The tragedy of old age is not that one is old, but that one is young.

—Oscar Wilde, *The Picture of Dorian Gray*

The pulse of joy that beats in us at twenty becomes sluggish. Our limbs fail, our senses rot. We degenerate into hideous puppets, haunted by the memory of the passions of which we were too much afraid, and the exquisite temptations that we had not the courage to yield to. Youth! Youth! There is absolutely nothing in the world but youth!

—Oscar Wilde, *The Picture of Dorian Gray*

I have just come back from a children's party. I am one of the survivors. There are not many of us.

—Percy French

The old believe everything; the middle-aged suspect everything; the young know everything.

—Oscar Wilde

The perfect age for children: Too old to cry at night and too young to borrow the car.

—Tatler in the *Irish Independent*

OVERHEARD IN DUBLIN

WOMAN #1: My young Paddy was sent home from school yesterday 'cause the lad sittin' next to him was smoking.

WOMAN #2: And why was your lad sent home then?

WOMAN #1: Well, I think that it was Paddy that set him on fire.

The condition of perfection is idleness; the aim of perfection is youth.

—Oscar Wilde, "Phrases and Philosophies for the Use of the Young"

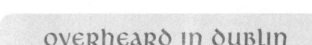

OVERHEARD IN DUBLIN

WOMAN #1: I nearly murdered my two young fellas last night, Bridie. There they were playing bridge in me good room.

WOMAN #2: And, sure what's wrong with that?

WOMAN #1: Well, one of them was between me two good chairs and the other fella was walking on top of him.

chapter 4

family

Fathers should be neither seen nor heard; that
is the only proper basis for family life.

—Oscar Wilde

*An old woman of the house discussing the arrival of
a new daughter-in-law:*
Ay, isn't it a dreadful thing to think of a strange
woman puttin' her hand into your tay cannister.

Children begin by loving their parents. After a
time they judge them. Rarely, if ever, do they
forgive them.

—Oscar Wilde, *A Woman of No Importance*

Few parents nowadays pay any regard to what
children say to them. The old-fashioned respect
for the young is fast dying.

—Oscar Wilde, *The Importance of Being Earnest*

A shoemaker's wife and a smith's mare are always badly shod.

—Traditional

♣

Extraordinary thing about the lower classes in England—they are always losing their relations. They are extremely fortunate in that respect.

—Oscar Wilde, *An Ideal Husband*

OVERHEARD IN DUBLIN

WOMAN #1: Isn't her babby lovely, Bridie? He looks just like his father.
WOMAN #2: Wouldn't it be better now, luv, if the child looked more like her husband.

To lose one parent...may be regarded as a misfortune; to lose both looks like carelessness.

—Oscar Wilde, *The Importance of Being Earnest*

I was influenced by my mother. Every man is when he is young.

—Oscar Wilde, *A Woman of No Importance*

overheard in dublin

"...and then the husband says to her, 'I'd like to be present at the birth of the baby.' 'Better for you,' says she, 'if you'd been there at the conception.'"

The best way to make children is to make them happy.

—Oscar Wilde

❧

After bringing a friend back to his Merrion Square house:
I want to introduce you to my mother. We have founded a Society for the Suppression of Virtue.

—Oscar Wilde

OVERHEARD IN DUBLIN

WOMAN #1: Yer man's a right eejit. I asked him what would he do if a foreigner tried to rape his sister and do you know what he said to me?
WOMAN #2: Wha'?
WOMAN #1: He said he'd try and get in between them.

Give a boy and a pig everything they want. You'll get a good pig and a bad boy.

—Traditional

chapter 5

RAGS
to
RICHES

Philanthropy seems to me to have become simply the refuge of people who wish to annoy their fellow creatures.

—Oscar Wilde, *An Ideal Husband*

♣

Spare a copper, sir, I am face to face with an empty stomach.

—Irish Beggar

He'd skin a flea for its hide and tallow.

—Traditional

Cecily: When I see a spade I call it a spade.
Gwendolene: I am glad to say I have never seen a spade. It is obvious that our social spheres have been widely different.

—Oscar Wilde, *The Importance of Being Earnest*

The Hon. Denis O'Connor went into a draper's shop,
and asked the price of a pair of gloves that took his
fancy. Thinking the price too high he exclaimed:
I'd sooner let my hands go barefoot for the rest
of my life.

♣

Charity creates a multitude of sins.

—Oscar Wilde

♣

When I was at Leadville and reflected that all the
shining silver that I saw coming from the mines
would be made into ugly dollars, it made me sad.

—Oscar Wilde

♣

It is better to have a permanent income than to be
fascinating.

—Oscar Wilde, "The Model Millionaire"

In court, Oscar Wilde's habit of giving acquaintances cigarette cases was suggested as being 'expensive if indulged in indiscriminately'. He replied:
Less expensive than giving jewelled garters to ladies.

In wealth, many friends. In poverty not even relatives.

—Traditional

Crime in England is rarely the result of sin. It is nearly always the result of starvation.

—Oscar Wilde, "Pen, Pencil and Poison"

OVERHEARD IN DUBLIN

MAN: I've heard that ye'r givin' up the stall, that ye've loads of money now.
WOMAN: Oh, indeed, I've enough money to last me a lifetime, that's if I don't spend anything.

The typical spendthrift is always giving away what he needs most.

—Oscar Wilde, *Vera, or The Nihilists*

Money talks, but you can't hold on to it long enough to start a conversation.

—*Dublin Opinion*

He rides in the Row at ten o'clock in the morning, goes to the Opera three times a week, changes his clothes at least five times a day, and dines out every night of the season. You don't call that leading an idle life, do you?

—Oscar Wilde, *An Ideal Husband*

Thim tha' has no cow, kin loss no cow.

—*Poor Rabbin's Ollminic*

Memory: Something a man forgets with when he owes you money.

—Traditional

♣

Time is waste of money.

—Oscar Wilde, "Phrases and Philosophies
for the Use of the Young"

♣

Once in a Dublin pub Brendan Behan was asked for a loan of a fiver by a gentleman with a nose for suckers. But Brendan was having none of it. 'I remember the time, Behan, when you hadn't a light' said the toucher. Behan replied:
That may be, but you don't remember it half as well as I do!

♣

Gold-tipped cigarettes are awfully expensive. I can only afford them when I am in debt.

—Oscar Wilde, *A Woman of No Importance*

It is very vulgar to talk about one's business. Only people like stockbrokers do that, and then merely at dinner parties.

—Oscar Wilde, *The Importance of Being Earnest*

OVERHEARD IN DUBLIN

"Well, hasn't he come up in the world, luv. It must be a great change for him to be reading a newspaper instead of eating his dinner offa it."

A super salesman: A man who sells something he hasn't got to people who don't want it.

—Traditional

On a co-operative association:
A combination of men with no money who meet each week to distribute it.

—J.C. Percy

Young people, nowadays, imagine that money is everything, and when they grow older they know it.

—Oscar Wilde, *The Picture of Dorian Gray*

overheard in dublin

"Oh, he says he won't leave them anythin.' Sure he's so mean that he'd live in yer ear and sub-let yer eardrum. Ye know, he'll probably turn it into travellers' cheques and take it with him."

Ordinary riches can be stolen from a man. Real riches cannot. In the treasure-house of your soul, there are infinitely precious things that may not be taken from you.

—Oscar Wilde, "The Soul of Man Under Socialism"

♣

A Dublin firm sent the following letter to customers whose accounts were overdue:
Man is dust. Dust settles. Be a man.

Nowadays we are all of us so hard up that the only pleasant things to pay are compliments. They're the only things we can pay.

—Oscar Wilde, *Lady Windermere's Fan*

I don't want money. It is people who pay their bills who want that, and I never pay mine.

—Oscar Wilde, *The Picture of Dorian Gray*

There are many things that we would throw away, if we were not afraid that others might pick them up.

—Oscar Wilde, *The Picture of Dorian Gray*

We live in an age when unnecessary things are our only necessities.

—Oscar Wilde

Richard Brinsley Sheridan, who was always in money troubles, was asked by a creditor to pay at least the interest on the money he owed. He replied:
My dear fellow, it is not in my interest to pay the principle or in my principle to pay the interest.

A toast! May our country one day become as prosperous as the Income Tax men think it is.

—*Dublin Opinion*

A Meath farmer's wife collected five thousand pounds insurance on her husband's death. When she was presented with the cheque she sighed:
Oh, dear, I'd give a thousand pounds to have my poor, dear husband back.

It is only by not paying one's bills that one can hope to live in the memory of the commercial classes.

> —Oscar Wilde, "Phrases and Philosophies
> for the Use of the Young"

An Irish beggar's coat: A bundle of holes sewn together.

> —Traditional

As for begging it is safer to beg than to take, but it is finer to take than to beg.

> —Oscar Wilde, "The Soul of Man Under Socialism"

OVERHEARD IN DUBLIN

WOMAN #1: I believe her husband has finally got work.

WOMAN #2: Yea, I heard he's selling furniture and they say they're down now to the bed.

I should fancy that the real tragedy of the poor is that they can afford nothing but self-denial.

—Oscar Wilde, *The Picture of Dorian Gray*

♣

I hand my pay packet to the wife every week, but I think she'd rather have the money.

—*The Bamba Review*

♣

There is only one class in the community that thinks more about money than the rich, and that is the poor. The poor can think of nothing else.

—Oscar Wilde, "The Soul of Man Under Socialism"

♣

What between the duties expected of one during one's lifetime, and the duties exacted from one after one's death, land has ceased to be either a profit or a pleasure.

—Oscar Wilde, *The Importance of Being Earnest*

College Green—where the orator Edmund Burke looks across at the Bank of Ireland, and only the money talks.

—Dublin Opinion

Credit is the capital of a younger son.

—Oscar Wilde, *The Picture of Dorian Gray*

fights
and
wars

Help a woman and hit a man.

—An Irish warriors proverb

♣

Reason won't stop the next war. It's easier to
explode an atom bomb than to explode a fallacy.

—*Dublin Opinion*

♣

Some Southern Americans have a melancholy
tendency to date every event of importance
by the late war. 'How beautiful the moon is tonight,'
I once remarked to a gentleman standing near me.
'Yes,' was his reply, 'but you should have seen it
before the war.'

—Oscar Wilde

♣

Advice to a novice:
There's no use in life in a man learning to fight
unless nature gave him a bit of a taste for it.

—Dan Donnelly

I don't know what effect they will have on the enemy, but by heaven they inspire me with terror!

—An Irish peer of a fighting unit

Wherever Brendan Behan went a large crowd went too and there was always the fellow who 'knew' him. On one occasion a noisy Kerryman shouted: 'We were in the same brigade in the IRA'. Behan sobered up and took a long look at the newcomer and said:
Go 'long, you bowsie, the only brigade you ever saw was the fire brigade.

I like to do all the talking myself. It saves time and prevents arguments.

—Oscar Wilde, "The Remarkable Rocket"

Murder is always a mistake...One should never do anything that one cannot talk about after dinner.

—Oscar Wilde, *The Picture of Dorian Gray*

To see a policeman running is, I think, next to hearing a declaration of war, the most exciting experience of which a human being is capable.

—Robert Lynd

OVERHEARD IN DUBLIN

MAN: Have ye got a paper, son?
PAPER BOY: There ye are, mister.
MAN: Are ye sure, now, this isn't yesterday's?
PAPER BOY: Careful, now, or ye might be in tomorrow's yerself.

To a wounded soldier:
What are you kicking up such a terrible row over? You would think that there was no one killed but yourself.

—Another wounded Cork soldier

Elizabeth Fitzgerald, surrounded by a vicious army of a neighbouring tribe in the sixteenth century, was told that her husband had been captured and unless she surrendered her castle immediately he would be hanged. She stood at the battlements and shouted back:
Mark these words, they may serve your own wives on some occasion. I'll keep my castle; for Elizabeth Fitzgerald may get another husband but Elizabeth Fitzgerald may never get another castle!

Thim tha' fights last fights best.

—*Poor Rabbin's Ollminic*

It is only the intellectually lost who ever argue.

—Oscar Wilde

Mr. Scully from Tipperary was the Whig candidate, and the family was not popular in its own county. A Cork-man, making inquiries of a Tipperary man about him, was answered:
I don't know this gentleman personally, but I believe we have already shot the best of the family.

— Samuel M. Hussy, *Reminiscences of an Irish Land Agent*

♣

Louis XIV once complained that his notorious Irish Brigade gave him more trouble than all his army put together. One of its officers spoke up:
Please, Your Majesty, your enemies make just the same complaint about us.

♣

Epigram on the building of a magazine for arms and stores:
Behold a proof of Irish sense;
Here Irish wit is seen;
When nothing's left that's worth defence,
They build a magazine.

—Dean Jonathan Swift

On the Cork Militia:
They are useless in times of war and dangerous in times of peace.

—Anonymous

♣

An Irish pilot serving in the RAF, as a piece of flak went through the fuselage on a raid over Germany:
Thank God Dev kept us out of this bloody war!

♣

two Dublin men were discussing the state of the country. 'The only hope for the country is for us to declare war on the United States,' said one. 'Why so?' asked the other. 'Because they would beat the tar out of us and then, following their usual custom they would be so sorry about it that they would send over millions of dollars to reconstruct the country. And then we'd be better off than we ever were before.' The other fellow took a long draught from his glass and seemed deep in thought. Then he asked: 'But where would we be if we won?'

—John Costello, former Taoiseach

> # Arguments are to be avoided; they are always vulgar and often convincing.
>
> —Oscar Wilde

Irish soldier: Can I take leave, sir, because my wife is in hospital and there is no one to look after the children.

CO: That's strange for I have here a letter from your wife saying that on no account was I to let you home, for every time you go you frighten herself and the children.

Irish soldier: Faith, there's two of the best liars in the army in this room. I was never married in me life.

I like talking to a brick wall; it's the only thing in the world that never contradicts me.

—Oscar Wilde, *Lady Windermere's Fan*

Epitaph:
Erected to the memory of John Moran, accidentally shot as a mark of affection by his brother.

♣

After a victorious battle:
General: Well my good fellow, and what did you do to help us to gain this victory?
Soldier: Do? Well, sir, I walked up boldly to one of the enemy, and cut off his feet.
General: Cut off his feet! Why did you not cut off his head?
Soldier: Ah! and faith, that was off already.

> He that wrestles strengthens our nerves and sharpens our skill. Our antagonist is our helper.

—Edmund Burke

Returned Irish soldier to the gaping crowd, as he exhibited with some pride his tall hat with a bullet hole in it: See there! Look at that hole, will you? Ye see, if it had been a low-crowned hat, I should have been killed outright.

🍀

I can stand brute force, but brute reason is quite unbearable. There is something unfair about its use. It is hitting below the intellect.

—Oscar Wilde

🍀

While retreating:
Soldier 1: Come on, Jack Dargan.
Soldier 2: I can't.
Soldier 1: Why not?
Soldier 2: I've taken a prisoner.
Soldier 1: Bring him with you.
Soldier 2: He won't come.
Soldier 1: Then come without him.
Soldier 2: He won't let me.

Three men were in hiding waiting to ambush Lord Leitrim, who was renowned not only for his brutality but also for his punctuality: 'He's late tonight,' said one of the men. Another replied:
I hope to God nothing's happened to the poor gentleman.

An Irish recruit being rebuked by his sergeant for striking one of his companions apologised:
I thought there was no harm in it, sergeant, all I had in me hand was me fist.

Arguments are extremely vulgar, for everybody in good society holds exactly the same opinions.

—Oscar Wilde

Gentleman: Pat, what's all that noise in the street?
Servant: Oh, nothing, sir; they're only forcing a man to join the volunteers.

A quartermaster in a regiment of Light Horse, who was six feet tall and very corpulent, was joking with an Irishman concerning the natural proneness of his countrymen to make Bulls in conversation. The Irishman replied:

By my soul, Ireland never made such a Bull in all its lifetime as England did when she made a light horseman of you.

An Irishman is never at peace except when he is fighting.

—Anonymous

A soldier's defence for stealing his comrade's whiskey ration:

I'd be sorry indeed sir to be called a thief. I put the liquor in the same bottle his and mine, and mine was at the bottom, and, sure, I was obliged to drink his to get at mine.

Last Thursday notice was given that a gang of rebels were advancing here under the French standard. Fortunately the rebels had no guns, except pistols and pikes, and as we had plenty of muskets and ammunition we put them all to the sword. Not a soul of them escaped except some of them that were drowned in an adjacent bog; and in a very short time there was nothing to be heard but silence.

—Sir Boyle Roche

♣

A soldier was carrying a comrade suffering from a leg wound along the front line when unknown to him a shot knocked the comrade's head off. When the soldier got to the casualty station someone pointed out to him that the corpse lacked a head. The soldier said:
The deceiving creature, he told me it was his leg that was shot.

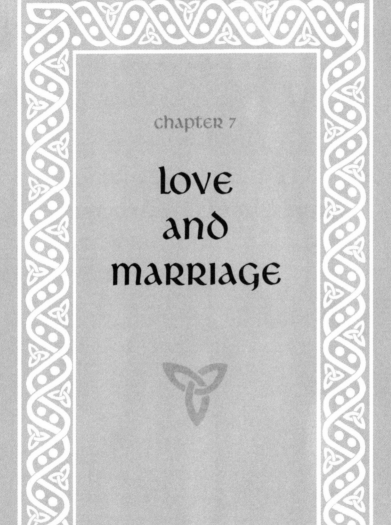

chapter 7

love
and
marriage

A beggar's blessing:
Long life to you, sir, and may you never see your
wife a widow.

Keep your eyes wide open before marriage and half shut afterwards.

—Anonymous

Nowadays all the married men are like bachelors,
and all the bachelors like married men.

—Oscar Wilde, *The Picture of Dorian Gray*

I don't think there is a woman in the world who
would not be a little flattered if one made love to
her. It is that which makes women so irresistibly
adorable.

—Oscar Wilde, *A Woman of No Importance*

An Irishman complaining of the hazards of marriage:
If I had my time to come again I would never marry
so young even if I lived to the age of Methuselah.

🍀

Irish proposal of marriage:
How would you like to be buried with my people?

🍀

She'll never love you unless you are always at her
heels; women like to be bothered.

—Oscar Wilde, *Vera,* or *The Nihilists*

OVERHEARD IN DUBLIN

MAN: Do you want a ride on me Suzuki?
WOMAN: Suzuki? Jaysus, I never heard it called
that before.

Plain women are always jealous of their husbands.
Beautiful women never have time. They are always
so occupied in being jealous of other people's husbands.

—Oscar Wilde, *A Woman of No Importance*

🍀

It is a curious thing about the game of marriage—
the wives hold all the honours, and invariably lose
the odd trick.

—Oscar Wilde, *Lady Windermere's Fan*

🍀

Respect is love in plain clothes.

—Frankie Byrne

🍀

*Parthelon, a leader in ancient Ireland, found his wife
in another man's arms. His wife faced him:*
O Parthelon, do you think it is possible for a child
and cake, a cat and milk, a bee and honey, or a
man and woman to be left alone with one another
without them meddling with one another?

Where there is no exaggeration there is no love, and where there is no love there is no understanding.

—Oscar Wilde

Courtship: A period during which a girl decides whether she can do better or not.

—Traditional

As a rule, people who act lead the most common-place lives. They are good husbands or faithful wives, or something tedious.

—Oscar Wilde, *The Picture of Dorian Gray*

Women give to men the very gold of their lives. But they invariably want it back in small change.

—Oscar Wilde

There is only one real tragedy in a woman's life.
The fact that her past is always her lover, and her
future invariably her husband.

—Oscar Wilde, *An Ideal Husband*

It is perfectly brutal the way most women nowadays
behave to men who are not their husbands.

—Oscar Wilde, *Lady Windermere's Fan*

Love is the soul of the neat Irishman;
He loves all that's lovely, And loves all he can.

—Traditional Irish song

People are either hunting for husbands or hiding from them.

—Oscar Wilde, *An Ideal Husband*

I am sick of women who love me. Women who hate me are much more interesting.

—Oscar Wilde, *The Picture of Dorian Gray*

OVERHEARD IN DUBLIN

"Well, mister, are ye goin' to buy them vegetables or do you have to ask yer wife for your opinion?"

In the case of very fascinating women, sex is a challenge, not a defence."

—Oscar Wilde, *An Ideal Husband*

When a woman marries again, it is because she detested her first husband. When a man marries again, it is because he adored his first wife. Women try their luck; men risk theirs.

—Oscar Wilde, *The Picture of Dorian Gray*

marriage is the earliest fruit of civilisation and it will be the latest. I think a man and a woman should choose each other for life, for the simple reason that a long life with all its accidents is barely long enough for a man and woman to understand each other; and in this case, to understand is to love. The man who understands one woman is qualified to understand pretty well anything.

—John Butler Yeats

❦

Men marry because they are tired; women because they are curious; both are disappointed.

—Oscar Wilde, *The Picture of Dorian Gray*

❦

A Dublin university professor speaking on the Catholic Church's attitude to sex in 1967:
The religious teaching on sex is seen as one which offers a woman a choice between perpetual virginity and perpetual pregnancy.

For an artist to marry his model is as fatal as for a gourmet to marry his cook; the one gets no sittings, and the other no dinners.

—Oscar Wilde

Modern women understand everything except their husbands.

—Oscar Wilde

No man should have a secret from his wife—she invariably finds it out.

—Oscar Wilde

♣

The one charm of marriage is that it makes a life of deception absolutely necessary for both parties.

—Oscar Wilde, *The Picture of Dorian Gray*

Some of our struggling countrymen have, with a small stock of learning and vigorous constitution, crept into the arms of many a fine woman and an affluent fortune.

—*The Irish Register*

♣

The subject being discussed was mistletoe. A woman turned to Father Healy and said, 'This, of course, does not interest you, Father.' He replied:
No, not really, we do it sub rosa.

OVERHEARD IN DUBLIN

WOMAN #1: I'll tell ye, Bridie, I'm totally against divorce. Why should anyone get off what I've had to suffer for the last twenty years?
WOMAN #2: Well, I'll tell ye one thing, if ye had killed him on the honeymoon, ye'd be out be now.

The happiness of a married man depends on the people he has not married.

—Oscar Wilde, *A Woman of No Importance*

The best way to look at the faults of a pretty woman: Close your eyes.

—Anonymous

The husbands of very beautiful women belong to the criminal classes.

—Oscar Wilde, *The Picture of Dorian Gray*

I have often observed that in married households the champagne is rarely of a first-rate brand.

—Oscar Wilde, *The Importance of Being Earnest*

The amount of women in London who flirt with their own husbands is perfectly scandalous. It looks so bad. It is simply washing one's clean linen in public.

—Oscar Wilde, *The Importance of Being Earnest*

One should always be in love. That is the reason one should never marry.

—Oscar Wilde

If we men married the women we deserve we should have a very bad time of it.

—Oscar Wilde, *An Ideal Husband*

Woman: Do you know who I am? I'm the Bishop's lady.
Shop assistant: I'm sorry ma'am, but I can't give you a discount even if you were his wife.

OVERHEARD IN DUBLIN

MAN #1: Hey, mister, why did ye get the dog?
MAN #2: Oh, I got it for the wife.
MAN #1: Jaysus, ye made a good bargain there.

Mrs. Allonby: My husband is a sort of promissory note; I'm tired of meeting him.

—Oscar Wilde, *A Woman of No Importance*

There's nothing in the world like the devotion of a married woman. It's a thing no married man knows anything about.

—Oscar Wilde, *Lady Windermere's Fan*

Irish bachelor justifying his distrust of marriage:
It took this country seven hundred years to get its freedom—I'm not going to give it up in five minutes!

OVERHEARD IN DUBLIN

WOMAN #1: Mary, how many husbands has that wan had?

WOMAN #2: You mean apart from her own?

Men always want to be a woman's first love. That is their clumsy vanity. Women have a more subtle instinct about things; what they like is to be a man's last romance.

—Oscar Wilde, *A Woman of No Importance*

James Stephens once asked George Moore for advice on how to treat two women who would be sitting on either side of him at a formal dinner party:

Don't touch their knees, woman have an instinctive knowledge whether a man who touches her knee is caressing her or only wiping his greasy fingers on her stocking.

—George Moore

There is nothing so difficult to marry as a large nose.

—Oscar Wilde, *An Ideal Husband*

On Irishmen who marry late:
I have only four plausible explanations for Irish continence: that sexual desire is sublimated by religion, exhausted by sport, drugged by drink, or deflected by either an innate or inculcated puritanism.

—Sean O'Faolain

They do not sin at all / Who sin for love.

—Oscar Wilde, *The Duchess of Padua*

Men are horribly tedious when they are good husbands, and abominably conceited when they are not.

—Oscar Wilde, *A Woman of No Importance*

ear Miss, I have been in love with you for a long time, and take this opportunity to inform you by letter; and would ye like to cort for marriage? If so, I would like to have you if you are not spoke for. And if you are spoke for, is your sister spoke for? You and she is both so hansom it is hard to tell which is the hansomis. I have got a little farm, an' don't you think I am pretty good-looking. I think you are very good looking. And if you want me an' if you don't want me be sure an' answer me yes or no.

—Letter by a young Irish farmer

It is not the perfect but the imperfect who have need of love.

—Oscar Wilde, *An Ideal Husband*

A young Irishman led a blushing female into the presence of the genial Father Carpenter:
Young Irishman: We want to get married, are you Father Carpenter?
Father Carpenter: Yes. Carpenter and joiner.

When a man has once loved a woman, he will do anything for her, except continue to love her.

—Oscar Wilde

♣

Sean: How is your wife getting on, Pat?
Pat: Well, sometimes she's better and sometimes she's worse. But from her goin's on when she's better, I often think that she's better when she's worse.

♣

Love is an illusion.

—Oscar Wilde, *The Picture of Dorian Gray*

OVERHEARD IN DUBLIN

WOMAN #1: So, she's no longer married and unhappy then?
WOMAN #2: No, luv, now she's separated and grateful.

Romance is the privilege of the rich, not the profession of the poor.

—Oscar Wilde, "The Model Millionaire"

A man can be happy with any woman as long as he does not love her.

—Oscar Wilde, *The Picture of Dorian Gray*

Marriage, which is the oldest form of association in human history, has never been perfect, is still imperfect and will always be unsatisfactory. Yet it is our most popular and our happiest wrong.

—St. John Ervine

The very essence of romance is uncertainty. If ever I get married, I'll certainly try to forget the fact.

—Oscar Wilde, *The Importance of Being Earnest*

Once a week is quite enough to propose to anyone, and it should always be done in a manner that attracts some attention.

—Oscar Wilde, *An Ideal Husband*

OVERHEARD IN DUBLIN

MAN #1: He says his wife is an angel.
MAN #2: Jaysus, he's lucky. I didn't know she was dead yet.

It's a lonely washing that hasn't a man's shirt in it.

—Anonymous

Father Keegan: The more a man knows, and the farther he travels, the more likely he is to marry a country girl afterwards.

—George Bernard Shaw, *John Bull's Other Island*

A Belfast woman summoned her husband for assault.
She said he was drunk. He said she was lazy and good
for nothing and hadn't given him a decent meal for over
a week:

Wife: You're a liar as well, that I did.

Husband: You did not, an' I can prove it. I pawned the gas stove last Tuesday and you haven't missed it yet.

OVERHEARD IN DUBLIN

WOMAN #1: I hear her parents are goin' with them on the honeymoon.

WOMAN #2: And does she mind?

WOMAN #1: Oh no, sure she says it'll be great havin' someone to mind the child.

I am not at all romantic. I am not old enough.
I leave romance to my seniors.

—Oscar Wilde, *An Ideal Husband*

Marriage is the one subject on which all women agree and all men disagree.

—Oscar Wilde

Her capacity for family affection is extraordinary. When her third husband died, her hair turned quite gold from grief.

—Oscar Wilde, *The Picture of Dorian Gray*

mr. O'Flaherty: I presume, Mrs. Murphy, you carry a memento of some sort in that locket of yours?

Mrs. Murphy: Indeed I do, sir; it's a lock of my Dan's hair.

Mr. O'Flaherty: But your husband is still alive.

Mrs. Murphy: Yes, sir, but his hair is all gone.

If one really loves a woman, all other women in the world become absolutely meaningless to one.

—Oscar Wilde, *Lady Windermere's Fan*

Parents had just made a match between their son and the daughter of a well-to-do local farmer. The couple had never met and after the first bringing together the son complained to the father: 'You never told me she was lame'. The father replied:

Go on outa that, it isn't for racing that you want her!

Who, being loved, is poor?

—Oscar Wilde, *A Woman of No Importance*

Nothing spoils a romance so much as a sense of humour in the woman—or the want of it in the man.

—Oscar Wilde, *A Woman of No Importance*

Divorces are made in heaven.

—Oscar Wilde

One can always recognise women who trust their husbands; they look so thoroughly unhappy.

—Oscar Wilde

overheard in dublin

MAN: Hey, missus, will that plant grow anywhere?
WOMAN: Indeed it will, son, sure 'tis like love-making, you can have it in a bed or up against the wall.

Those who are faithful know only the trivial side of love: it is the faithless who know love's tragedies.

—Oscar Wilde, *The Picture of Dorian Gray*

OVERHEARD IN DUBLIN

WOMAN #1: Well, Maisie told me that she's havin' no more, that she's going to practise birth control.
WOMAN #2: Jaysus, luv, her best birth control would be to leave the lights on.

When the henpecked husband died and went below, he immediately started throwing his weight around and giving orders to everyone:
Satan: Say, fellow you're acting as though you owned the place.
Husband: I do! My wife gave it to me while I was on earth.

♣

If you marry the right woman there is nothing like it and if you marry the wrong woman there is nothing like it.

—Traditional

An Irish couple, whose married bliss was not without a few squalls, received a homely lecture from their spiritual adviser regarding their disgraceful quarrels:

Pastor: Why, the dog and cat you have agree better than you.

Husband: If your reverence'll tie them together, ye'll soon change yer mind.

♣

Teacher: So your name is Johnny Murphy, But your mother's name is O'Brien?

Student: Yes ma'am. You see, she married again and I didn't.

> Polygamy—how much more poetic it is to marry one and love many.
>
> —Oscar Wilde

Jimmy Hiney, Ireland's great ballad writer, tells this story about himself. A small man, he was taken home to meet his mother-in-law who, looking at him with amazement on her face, said to her daughter:
Well begod if you get nothing else from him you'll always get a laugh.

A kiss may ruin a human life.

—Oscar Wilde, *A Woman of No Importance*

This is a woman's world. When a man is born people ask, 'How is the mother?' When he marries they exclaim, 'What a beautiful bride.' When he dies they inquire, 'How much did he leave her?'

—Anonymous

🍀

The only difference between a caprice and a life-long passion is that the caprice lasts a little longer.

—Oscar Wilde, *The Picture of Dorian Gray*

Marriage is hardly a thing that one can do now and then—except in America.

—Oscar Wilde, *The Picture of Dorian Gray*

♣

All men are married women's property. That is the only true definition of what married women's property really is.

—Oscar Wilde, *A Woman of No Importance*

♣

There is no such thing as confirmed bachelors up to the age of fifty-two—only obstinate ones.

—Traditional

OVERHEARD IN DUBLIN

MAN: Hey, Rosie, I'll say this much for ye, ye bring out the animal in me.
WOMAN: Jaysus, keep away from me, luv, I've always been afraid of mice.

First love is only a little foolishness and a lot of curiosity. No really self-respecting woman would take advantage of it.

—George Bernard Shaw

OVERHEARD IN DUBLIN

WOMAN #1: Josie told me that she was going to have the coil inserted.

WOMAN #2: Jesus, luv, with her that's like locking the stable door after the horse has bolted.

Mrs. Cheveky: Their husbands. That is the one thing the modern woman never understands.
Lady Markby: And a very good thing too, dear, I dare say. It might break up many a happy home if they did.

—Oscar Wilde, *An Ideal Husband*

Mike: Say, Mrs. Nolan, I hear you are keeping company with a man, an' your husband is only dead six months.

Widow Nolan: True for you, Mike, I am, an' glad of it.

Mike: Sure, I am ashamed to hear you say so, and indeed you ought to have more respect for his memory.

Widow Nolan: Whist, now, Mike; you can't take a memory in your arms of a cold night.

Never take for a wife a woman who has no faults.

—Traditional

Women have been so highly educated that nothing should surprise them except happy marriages.

—Oscar Wilde

Twenty years of romance make a woman look like a ruin; but twenty years of marriage make her look like a public building.

—Oscar Wilde, *A Woman of No Importance*

♣

How marriage ruins a man! It's as demoralising as cigarettes, and far more expensive.

—Oscar Wilde, *Lady Windermere's Fan*

The proper basis for marriage is a mutual misunderstanding.

—Oscar Wilde, "Lord Arthur Savile's Crime"

Marriage: A pair of shears that cannot be separated, often moving in opposite directions, yet always punishing whatever comes between them.

—Traditional

Young men want to be faithful and are not; old men want to be faithless and cannot.

—Oscar Wilde, *The Picture of Dorian Gray*

OVERHEARD IN DUBLIN

WOMAN #1: Are they pleased that the babby's on the way now?
WOMAN #2: Oh, they're so pleased now, luv, that they're plannin' to get married.

A man who desires to get married should know either everything or nothing.

—Oscar Wilde

The Belfast man wanted a good-looking girl:
'I'd like to marry a girl that is the full o' me eye.'

—*Poor Rabbin's Ollminic*

chapter 8

on
beauty

It is only the shallow people who do not judge by appearances.

—Oscar Wilde, *The Picture of Dorian Gray*

♣

It is better to be beautiful than to be good, but it is better to be good than to be ugly.

—Oscar Wilde

♣

To be pretty is the best fashion there is, and the only fashion that England succeeds in setting.

—Oscar Wilde, *An Ideal Husband*

♣

Going into a florist's shop in Jermyn Street, Oscar Wilde asked for several bunches of flowers to be removed from the window. 'With pleasure, sir. How many would you like to have?' asked the assistant. He replied:
Oh, I don't want any, thank you. I only asked to have them removed from the window because I thought that they looked tired.

overheard in dublin

WOMAN #1: You're a bit down today, Chrissie,
what's up with ye?
WOMAN #2: Well, I'm wondering that as I get older
will I start to lose me looks?
WOMAN #1: Well, ye will, luv, if ye'r lucky.

I consider ugliness a kind of malady, and illness and
suffering always inspire me with revulsion. A man
with the toothache ought, I know, to have my
sympathy, for it is a terrible pain, yet he fills me
with nothing but aversion.

—Oscar Wilde

♣

The only way to behave to a woman is to make love
to her, if she is pretty, and to someone else, if she is
plain.

—Oscar Wilde, *The Importance of Being Earnest*

'I propose,' said Dean Jonathan Swift to a group
of friends, 'that a tax be levied on female beauty.'
'But, sir,' objected a listener, 'could we ever make
women pay enough to make such a tax levy
worth while?'
'That would be the least of our difficulties,' laughed
Swift. 'Let every woman be permitted to assess her
own charms—then she'll be generous enough.'

🍀

I don't mind plain women being Puritans. It is the
only excuse they have for being plain.

—Oscar Wilde, *A Woman of No Importance*

OVERHEARD IN DUBLIN

WOMAN #1: I don't think I look forty-two, Bridie,
do I?
WOMAN #2: No, luv, but ye used to.

Benoît Constant Coquelin: What is civilisation, M. Wilde?

Oscar Wilde: Love of beauty.

Coquelin: And what is beauty?

Wilde: That which the bourgeois call ugly.

Coquelin: And what do the bourgeois call beautiful?

Wilde: It does not exist.

♣

Oscar Wilde met a woman in Paris who took a pride in her ugliness. 'Don't you think,' she asked him, 'that I am the ugliest woman in Paris?' He replied:

No—in all the world.

OVERHEARD IN DUBLIN

MAN: Hey, Maisie, you've a great pair of headlights there.

WOMAN: Well, son, isn't it better than having two flat tyres up front?

chapter 9

intelligence
and
stupidity

The well-bred contradict other people. The wise
contradict themselves.

—Oscar Wilde, "Phrases and Philosophies
for the Use of the Young"

There is always more brass than brains in an
aristocracy.

—Oscar Wilde, *Vera, or The Nihilists*

The wise are polite all the world over—but fools are polite only at home.

—Oliver Goldsmith

The public have an insatiable curiosity to know
everything, except what is worth knowing.

—Oscar Wilde, "The Soul of Man Under Socialism"

OVERHEARD IN DUBLIN

WOMAN #1: This fella comes over to me. 'Is it possible to buy half a head of cabbage, madam?' says he. 'Oh, I'll have to ask the boss about that,' says I, quickly. So I goes over to Paddy and I says, 'Paddy there's an oul' stupid ghet over there who wants to buy half a head of cabbage.' Well, merciful Jesus, didn't I turn round and there he was right behind me.

WOMAN #2: What did ye do?

WOMAN #1: 'Oh,' says I, 'and this nice gentleman will have the other half.'

I do not approve of anything that tampers with natural ignorance.

—Oscar Wilde

♣

There is no sin except stupidity.

—Oscar Wilde, "The Critic as Artist"

The public is wonderfully tolerant. It forgives everything except genius.

—Oscar Wilde, "The Critic as Artist"

It is only about the things that do not interest one that one can give an unbiased opinion; and this is no doubt the reason why an unbiased opinion is always valueless.

—Oscar Wilde

OVERHEARD IN DUBLIN

"You know she's that stupid that she took back the pill and told the doctor it was the wrong size, that it kept fallin' out."

It is always an advantage not to have received a sound commercial education.

—Oscar Wilde, "The Portrait of Mr. W.H."

The clever people never listen, and the stupid people never talk.

—Oscar Wilde, *A Woman of No Importance*

To do nothing at all is the most difficult thing in the world, the most difficult and the most intellectual.

—Oscar Wilde

Thinking is the most unhealthy thing in the world, and people die of it just as they die of any other disease. Fortunately, in England at any rate, thought is not catching. Our splendid physique as a people is entirely due to our national stupidity.

—Oscar Wilde, "The Decay of Lying"

Only dull people are brilliant at breakfast.

—Oscar Wilde, *An Ideal Husband*

Wisdom is a fox, who, after long hunting, will at last cost you the pains to dig it out; it is a cheese, which, by how much the richer, has the thicker, the homelier, and the coarser coat, and whereof to a judicious palate the maggots are the best; it is a sack-posset, wherein the deeper you go you will find it the sweeter. Wisdom is a hen, whose cackling we must value and consider, because it is attended with an egg; but then, lastly, it is a nut, which, unless you choose with judgment, may cost you a tooth, and pay you with nothing but a worm.

—Dean Jonathan Swift

Nowadays to be intelligible is to be found out.

—Oscar Wilde, *Lady Windermere's Fan*

There are only two kinds of people who are really fascinating—people who know absolutely everything and people who know absolutely nothing.

—Oscar Wilde, *The Picture of Dorian Gray*

Ignorance is like a delicate exotic fruit; touch it and the bloom is gone.

—Oscar Wilde

OVERHEARD IN DUBLIN

"That poor oul' wan is so unfortunate that if it was raining soup she'd be out with a fork."

Lady Basildon: Ah! I hate being educated!
Mrs. Marchmont: So do I. It puts one almost on a level with the commercial classes.

—Oscar Wilde, *An Ideal Husband*

Education is an admirable thing, but it is well to remember from time to time that nothing that is worth knowing can be taught.

—Oscar Wilde, "The Critic as Artist"

Caricature is the tribute mediocrity pays to genius.

—Oscar Wilde

He is a wise man who has his afterthoughts first.

—Traditional

Genius is born, not paid.

—Oscar Wilde

♣

In examinations the foolish ask questions that the wise cannot answer.

—Oscar Wilde , "Phrases and Philosophies for the Use of the Young"

♣

Wisdom comes with winters.

—Oscar Wilde, *A Florentine Tragedy*

When a true Genius appears in the world you may know him by this sign; that the Dunces are all in Confederacy against him.

—Dean Jonathan Swift

❧

Everybody who is incapable of learning has taken to teaching—that is really what our enthusiasm for education has come to.

—Oscar Wilde, "The Decay of Lying"

OVERHEARD IN DUBLIN

MAN #1: I don't know how yer wan manages to do so many bleedin' stupid things in the one day.
MAN #2: I think she must get up early, luv.

You can't go anywhere without meeting clever people. The thing has become an absolute public nuisance. I wish to goodness we had a few fools left.

—Oscar Wilde, The Importance of Being Earnest

chapter 10

nations around the world

Lady Carteret, wife of the Lord Lieutenant of Ireland: Sir, the air of your country is healthy and very excellent.
Dean Jonathan Swift: For God's sake, madam, don't say so in England; for if you do they will certainly tax it.

♣

The English have a miraculous power of turning wine into water.

—Oscar Wilde

♣

On London thoroughfares:
Wearied of the houses you turn to contemplate the street itself, you have nothing to look at but chimney-pot hats, men with sandwich boards, vermilion letter-boxes, and do that even at the risk of being run over by an emerald-green omnibus.

—Oscar Wilde

To fail and to die young is the only hope for a Scotsman who wishes to remain an artist.

—Oscar Wilde

The youth of America is their oldest tradition.
It has been going on now for three hundred years.
To hear them talk we would imagine they were
in their first childhood. As far as civilisation goes
they are in their second.

—Oscar Wilde

♣

Of course America had often been discovered
before Columbus, but it had always been hushed up.

—Oscar Wilde

The English think that a cheque can solve every problem in life.

—Oscar Wilde

All Americans lecture…I suppose it is something
in their climate.

—Oscar Wilde, *A Woman of No Importance*

American girls are as clever at concealing their parents as English women are at concealing their past.

—Oscar Wilde, *The Picture of Dorian Gray*

♣

To go to California and not see Hollywood is like going to Ireland and not seeing the Lakes of Killarney.

—Brendan Behan

♣

On American girls:
Pretty and charming—little oases of pretty unreasonableness in a vast desert of practical common sense.

—Oscar Wilde

♣

An Irishman's description of an American:
He'd kiss a queen till he'd raise a blister,
With his arms round her neck, and his old felt hat on;
Address a king by the title of Mister,
And ask him the price of the throne he sat on.

The cup of Ireland's miseries has been overflowing
for centuries and is not yet full.

—Sir Boyle Roche

♣

the crude commercialism of America, its
materialist spirit, its indifference to the poetical
side of things, and its lack of imagination and of
high unattainable ideals, are entirely due to that
country having adopted for its national hero a
man who, according to his own confession, was
incapable of telling a lie, and it is not too much to
say that the story of George Washington and the
cherry tree has done more harm, and in a shorter
space of time, than any other moral tale in the
whole of literature—and the amusing part of the
whole thing is that the story of the cherry tree is an
absolute myth.

—Oscar Wilde, "The Decay of Lying"

♣

Englishwomen conceal their feelings till after they
are married. They show them then.

—Oscar Wilde, A Woman of No Importance

To disagree with three-fourths of the British public on all points is one of the first elements of sanity, one of the deepest consolations in all moments of spiritual doubt.

—Oscar Wilde

Sound English common sense—the inherited stupidity of the race.

—Oscar Wilde

England will never be civilised until she has added Utopia to her dominions.

—Oscar Wilde, "The Critic as Artist"

I don't desire to change anything in England except the weather.

—Oscar Wilde, *The Picture of Dorian Gray*

If in the last century she [England] tried to govern Ireland with an insolence that was intensified by race hatred and religious prejudice, she has sought to rule her in this century with a stupidity that is aggravated by good intentions.

—Oscar Wilde

On being told that Rossetti, in order to get rid of a poet who was always cadging, had given him enough money to go to the States:
Of course, if one had the money to go to America, one would not go.

—Oscar Wilde

The English have really everything in common with the Americans, except, of course, language.

—Oscar Wilde

The great difference between England and Ireland
is that in England you can say what you like as long
as you do the right thing; in Ireland you can do
what you like as long as you say the right thing.

—Anonymous politician

♣

On the flooded, yellow, raging, hissing, rushing
Mississippi River:
No well-behaved river ought to act that way.

—Oscar Wilde

♣

Mrs. Cheveley: A typical Englishman, always dull
and usually violent.

—Oscar Wilde, *An Ideal Husband*

♣

On Niagara Falls:
Simply a vast unnecessary amount of water
going the wrong way and then falling over
unnecessary rocks.

—Oscar Wilde

The famous entertainer, Val Vousden, once asked a
circus master, who was playing the same town, to give
their historical drama Robert Emmet *a boost.*
The ringmaster was delighted to help and announced
during the evening:
If you want to see how Ireland has suffered and
is suffering still, go and see Val Vousden play
Robert Emmet!

♣

Tenant Right in Tipperary:
If the landlords and the police were abolished
there wouldn't be a nation like Ireland on the face
of the earth.

♣

I love London society! I think it has immensely
improved. It is entirely composed now of beautiful
idiots and brilliant lunatics. Just what society
should be.

—Oscar Wilde, *An Ideal Husband*

The Americans are certainly great hero-worshippers,
and always take their heroes from the criminal classes.

—Oscar Wilde

My one claim to originality among Irishmen is
that I have never made a speech.

—George Moore

Patriotism is the virtue of the vicious.

—Oscar Wilde

For the American:
Art has no marvel, and Beauty no meaning, and
the Past no message.

—Oscar Wilde

My father used to say, that the great difference between England and Ireland is that every Englishman has rich relations and every Irishman poor ones.

—William Butler Yeats

I need hardly say that we were delighted and amused at the typical English way in which our ideas were misunderstood. They took our epigrams as earnest, and our parodies as prose.

—Oscar Wilde

Ocean: Huge body of water surrounded entirely by rumours of everlasting peace.

—Anonymous

To a newspaperman in Cincinnati:
I wonder your criminals don't plead the ugliness
of your city as an excuse for their crimes.

—Oscar Wilde

🍀

The English can't stand a man who is always saying
he is right, but they are very fond of a man who
admits he has been in the wrong.

—Oscar Wilde, *An Ideal Husband*

🍀

Anyone who wishes to diminish the brotherly
affection of the two sister countries is an enemy
of both nations.

—Sir Boyle Roche

🍀

*Louis XIV asked Count Mahoney if he understood
Italian. He replied:*
Yes, please, Your Majesty, if it's spoken in Irish.

Sir Samuel Ferguson, the Belfast-born poet and antiquarian, visited Rath Cruaghan in Roscommon. He discussed the cromlech builders with the father of the famous entertainer, Percy French:

Old Mr. French: How a monolith, weighing one hundred tons, could be placed on pillars twelve feet high without the aid of machinery, I can't conceive.

Sir Samuel: An inclined plane, one thousand men, all pulling the same way would do it.

Old Mr. French: Granted, but where in Ireland would you find one thousand men all pulling the same way?

♣

After receiving a wire from Griggsville, Illionois asking Oscar Wilde to 'lecture us on aesthetics':

Begin by changing the name of your town.

—Oscar Wilde

♣

Overheard at an exhibition in Dublin of a model of an African village:

Thank God I was born at home.

If one could only teach the English how to talk,
and the Irish how to listen, society here would be
quite civilised.

—Oscar Wilde, *An Ideal Husband*

Nothing is impossible
in Russia but reform.

—Oscar Wilde, *Vera, or The Nihilists*

*In a violent anti-Home Rule speech in the House of
Commons in 1890:*
I was born Irish and have been so ever since.

—Colonel Saunderson, MP

Perhaps, after all, America never has been
discovered. I myself would say that it had merely
been detected.

—Oscar Wilde, *The Picture of Dorian Gray*

For a man to be both a genius and a Scotsman is
the very stage for tragedy…Your Scotsman believes
only in success…God saved the genius of Robert
Burns to poetry by driving him through drink
to failure.

—Oscar Wilde

In Paris one can lose one's time most delightfully; but one can never lose one's way.

—Oscar Wilde

I believe a serious problem for the American peo-
ple to consider is the cultivation of better manners.
It is the most noticeable, the most painful defect in
American civilisation.

—Oscar Wilde

The real weakness of England lies, not in incomplete armaments or unfortified coasts, not in the poverty that creeps through sunless lanes, or the drunkenness that brawls in loathsome courts, but simply in the fact that her ideals are emotional and not intellectual.

—Oscar Wilde, "The Critic as Artist"

Lord Caversham: Can't make out how you stand London society. The thing has gone to the dogs, a lot of damned nobodies talking about nothing.

—Oscar Wilde, *An Ideal Husband*

A Frenchman claiming for his country the invention of all the elegances, named among other things the ruffle. The Irishman answered: We went one better—we put the shirt on it.

If there were only three Irishmen left in the world you'd find two of them in a corner talking about the other. We're a backbiting race.

—Brendan Behan

In Ireland the inevitable never happens, but the unexpected often occurs.

—J.P. Mahaffy

The tourist in Ireland had seen the Devil's Gap, the Devil's Glen, and the Devil's Pot:
Tourist: The devil owns a lot of land in Ireland; he must be an important man.
Guide: You're right, but like all the landlords his home is in England.

A Russian who lives happily under the present system of government in Russia must either believe that man has no soul, or that, if he has, it is not worth developing.

—Oscar Wilde, "The Soul of Man Under Socialism"

Greek dress was in its essence inartistic. Nothing should reveal the body but the body.

—Oscar Wilde, "Phrases and Philosophies for the Use of the Young"

They [the English] insist in presenting us [the Irish] with all the good qualities they do not want for themselves.

—William Butler Yeats

When I look at the map and see what an ugly country Australia is, I feel that I want to go there and see if it cannot be changed into a more beautiful form!

—Oscar Wilde

🍀

The great superiority of France over England is that in France every bourgeois wants to be an artist, whereas in England every artist wants to be a bourgeois.

—Oscar Wilde

Flowers are as common in the country as people are in London.

—Oscar Wilde

In an Orange Day speech:
I look forward to the day when the British Lion
will march down the Shankill Road arm in arm
with the Statue of Liberty.

—Ulster MP

In England, at any rate, education produces no
effect whatsoever. If it did, it would prove a serious
danger to the upper classes, and would probably
lead to acts of violence in Grosvenor Square.

—Oscar Wilde, *The Importance of Being Earnest*

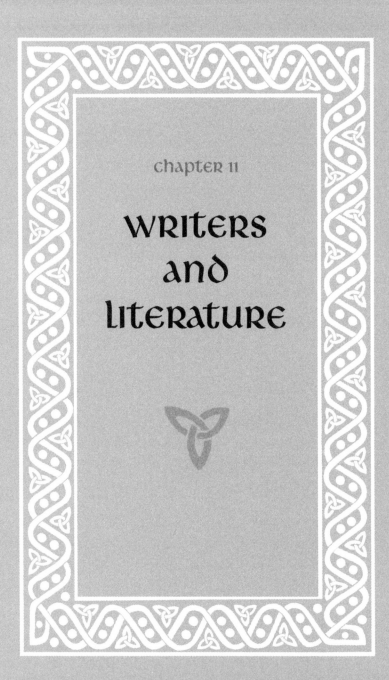

chapter 11

WRITERS
and
LITERATURE

*On a poet who wrote about a variety of
subjects, from popular watering-places and
universal providers to the immortality of the soul:*
We fear that he will never produce any real good
work till he has made up his mind whether destiny
intends him for a poet or for an advertising agent.

—Oscar Wilde

The basis of literary friendship is mixing the
poisoned bowl.

—Oscar Wilde

The only form of fiction in which real characters
do not seem out of place is history. In novels they
are detestable.

—Oscar Wilde

As he tossed a copy of Ulysses on the fire:
I could not write the words Mr. Joyce uses.

—George Bernard Shaw

When I was young I thought all the world, as well as myself, was wholly taken up in discoursing upon the last new play.

—Dean Jonathan Swift

♣

George Bernard Shaw once made a personal appearance at the end of one of his plays. When the general applause had subsided, one man began to hiss. Shaw immediately pointed his finger at the man:
I quite agree with you, my friend, it is a rotten play. But what are we among so many?

♣

To James Froude:
Like most penmen you overrate the power of the sword.

—Oscar Wilde

♣

Shilling literature is always making demands on our credulity without ever appealing to our imagination.

—Oscar Wilde

On a romantic novel:
It could be read without any trouble and was
probably written without any trouble also.

—Oscar Wilde

To William Butler Yeats on his fortieth birthday:
We have met too late, Mr. Yeats, you are too old
to be influenced by me.

—James Joyce

Oscar Wilde admitted to Arthur Conan Doyle:
Between me and life there is a mist of words
always. I throw probability out of the window for
the sake of a phrase, and the chance of an epigram
makes me desert truth. Still I do aim at making
a work of art.

On newspapers that had degenerated:
They may now be absolutely relied upon.

—Oscar Wilde

On publishing the poem "The Sphinx":
My first idea was to print only three copies; one
for myself, one for the British Museum, and one
for Heaven. I had some doubt about the British
Museum.

—Oscar Wilde

♣

Oscar Wilde's admiration for the academic evaporated
soon after university and he said that statements in a
book on Italian Literature demonstrated:
A want of knowledge that must be the result
of years of study.

♣

[George] Meredith is a prose [Robert] Browning
and so is Browning; he uses poetry as a medium for
writing prose.

—Oscar Wilde

George Bernard Shaw's flowing beard was long a topic of conversation:

Reporter: What made you grow a beard?

Shaw: Vanity, but common sense made me retain it.

Reporter: How is that?

Shaw: Well, in all these years, I've probably written several plays in the time I would have spent shaving.

It has been said to me that Mr. Moore had enough credulity to make him a bishop.

—Susan Mitchell

Wordsworth went to the lakes, but he was never a lake poet. He found in stones the sermons he had already hidden there.

—Oscar Wilde, "The Decay of Lying"

To James Joyce:
I don't know whether you are a mountain or a
cistern but I am afraid that you have not enough
chaos in you to make a world.

—AE (George Russell)

🍀

I never write plays for anyone. I write plays to
amuse myself. After, if people want to act in them,
I sometimes allow them to do so.

—Oscar Wilde

🍀

The aim of most of our modern novelists seems
to be, not to write good novels, but to write novels
that will do good.

—Oscar Wilde

🍀

Mr. Martyn and Mr. Moore are not writers of
much originality...Mr. Moore has wonderful
mimetic ability.

—James Joyce

I hate vulgar realism in literature. The man who could call a spade a spade should be compelled to use one. It is the only thing he is fit for.

—Oscar Wilde, *The Picture of Dorian Gray*

But there is no literary public in England for anything except newspapers, primers and encyclopaedias. Of all the people in the world the English have the least sense of the beauty of literature.

—Oscar Wilde, *The Picture of Dorian Gray*

In the foyer of the Cork House after the premiere of one of his plays, a lady with an umbrella stopped J. B. Keane and berated him publicly. 'Stand there,' she shouted, prodding him with the umbrella, 'till I give you a piece of my mind.' He responded:
My dear woman your mind is so small that if you give me a bit of it you wouldn't have any left for yourself.

The ancient historians gave us delightful fiction in the form of fact; the modern novelist presents us with dull facts under the guise of fiction.

—Oscar Wilde, "The Decay of Lying"

Journalism is unreadable, and literature is not read.

—Oscar Wilde, "The Critic as Artist"

One should not be too severe on English novels: they are the only relaxation of the intellectually unemployed.

—Oscar Wilde

♣

On Edward Martyn:
Moore's exotic bucolic.

—Robert Farren

On the amusing collaboration for Diarmuid and Grainne:
Moore was to write it in French; Lady Gregory would then translate his French into English; Taidg O'Donoghue would then translate the English into Irish and then Lady Gregory would translate the Irish into English! After that Yeats would put style upon it.

—George Moore

🍀

On how William Butler Yeats brought John Millington Synge to writing perfection:
He stood over him, his pearl pale, or is it his ivory hand, sweeping the strings of a harp of apple wood, rousing a masterpiece out of an abyss.

—George Moore

🍀

It is much more difficult to talk about a thing than to do it. In the sphere of actual life that is of course obvious. Anybody can make history. Only a great man can write it.

—Oscar Wilde, "The Critic as Artist"

Oscar Wilde confided to Vincent O'Sullivan:
Now when I start a thing I must write desperately
day and night till it is finished. Otherwise I should
lose interest in it, and the first bus passing in the
street would distract me from it.

I was working on the proof of one of my poems
all the morning, and took out a comma. In the
afternoon I put it back again.

—Oscar Wilde

On George Moore:
Moore suffered from mental diarrhea, which had
to be shot over his friends.

—Edward Martyn

No modern literary work of any worth has been
produced in English by an English writer—except
of course Bradshaw.

—Oscar Wilde

*On his refusal to read George Moore's famous malevo-
lent and entertaining trilogy,* Hail and Farewell:
George is a pleasant fellow to meet, and if I read
the book I might not be able to meet him again.

—Edward Martyn

I write because it gives me the greatest possible
artistic pleasure to write. If my work pleases the
few I am gratified. If it does not, it causes me no
pain. As for the mob, I have no desire to be a
popular novelist. It is far too easy.

—Oscar Wilde

In Hail and Farewell *George Moore reprinted some of
the French text from the play* Diarmuid and Grainne.
*His explanation was that it was the only
way he could convince the reader that:*
…Two such literary lunatics as Yeats and myself
existed, contemporaneously, and in Ireland, too.

The truth is rarely pure and never simple. Modern life would be very tedious if it were either, and modern literature a complete impossibility.

—Oscar Wilde, *The Importance of Being Earnest*

At twilight nature becomes a wonderfully suggestive effect, and is not without loveliness, though perhaps its chief use is to illustrate quotations from the poets.

—Oscar Wilde, "The Decay of Lying"

On Robert Yelverton Tyrrell:
If he had known less he would have been a poet.

—Oscar Wilde

Stephen Behan once explained why he did not produce plays like his two sons, Brendan and Dominic:
I've been too busy producing the playwrights.

Town life nourishes and perfects all the more civilised elements in man. Shakespeare wrote nothing but doggerel lampoon before he came to London and never penned a line after he left.

—Oscar Wilde

Swinburne is so eloquent that whatever he touches becomes unreal.

—Oscar Wilde

Any place you love is the world to you…but love is not fashionable any more: the poets have killed it. They wrote so much about it that nobody believed them, and I am not surprised.

—Oscar Wilde, "The Remarkable Rocket"

On George Moore's 'confession books', The Confessions of a Young Man *and* Memoirs of My Dead Life:

Some men kiss and tell; Moore tells but doesn't kiss.

—Sarah Purser

The critic is he who can translate into another manner of a new material his impression of beautiful things. The highest, as the lowest, form of criticism is a mode of autobiography.

—Oscar Wilde, *The Picture of Dorian Gray*

The books that the world calls immoral books are books that show the world its own shame.

—Oscar Wilde, *The Picture of Dorian Gray*

Lord Avebury had published his list of the "Hundred Best Books", and at a function where the views of celebrities were being canvassed Oscar Wilde was requested to compile a list of his hundred favourites. He replied:

I fear that would be impossible.

'But why?' he was asked.

Because I have only written five.

Literature always anticipates life. It does not copy it, but moulds it to its purpose. The nineteenth century, as we know it, is largely an invention of Balzac.

—Oscar Wilde, "The Decay of Lying"

Anybody can write a three-volumed novel. It merely requires a complete ignorance of both life and literature.

—Oscar Wilde, "The Critic as Artist"

On The Importance of Being Earnest:
The first act is ingenious, the second beautiful,
the third abominably clever.

—Oscar Wilde

All bad poetry springs from genuine feeling. To
be natural is to be obvious, and to be obvious is
to be inartistic.

—Oscar Wilde, "The Critic as Artist"

When Borstal Boy *was banned in Ireland, Brendan*
Behan tried to laugh it off and made up his own verse
to go to the tune of "MacNamara's Band":
Oh, me name is Brendan Behan, I'm the latest of
the banned,
Although we're small in numbers we're the best
banned in the land,
We're read at wakes and weddin's and in every
parish hall,
And under library counters sure you'll have no
trouble at all.

George Moore once wrote that his brother Maurice was the only member of his family who was a gentleman. Susan Mitchell replied:

Mr. Moore is an amazingly truthful person.

A poet can survive anything but a misprint.

—Oscar Wilde

We have been able to have fine poetry in England because the public do not read it, and consequently do not influence it.

—Oscar Wilde, "The Soul of Man Under Socialism"

In the old-fashioned novel the hero didn't kiss the heroine until the last page. Now he kisses her on the dust jacket.

—*Dublin Opinion*

Sir Walter Scott was travelling across an Irish ferry and put his hand in his pocket for sixpence for the ferryman. All he had was a shilling. 'Take it, Pat,' he said, 'and you'll give me the sixpence back another time'. The reply:

Sure, and may your honour live to get it.

Whistler, with all his faults, was never guilty of writing a line of poetry.

—Oscar Wilde

The tears that we shed at a play are a type of the exquisite sterile emotions that it is the function of Art to awaken. We weep but we are not wounded. We grieve but our grief is not bitter.

—Oscar Wilde, "The Critic as Artist"

George Bernard Shaw's Will:
He left his cash (God help typesetters!) to give the
alphabet more letters. Strange that he should on
forty fix who did so well with twenty-six!

—*Dublin Opinion*

♣

On Max Beerbohm:
The Gods bestowed on Max the gift of perpetual
old age.

—Oscar Wilde

♣

On Oscar Wilde:
Wilde paraphrased and inverted the witticisms and
epigrams of others. His method of literary piracy
was on the lines of the robber Cacus, who dragged
stolen cows backwards by the tails into his cavern
so that their hoofprints might not lead to detection.

—George Moore

I quite admit that modern novels have many good points. All I insist on is that, as a class, they are quite unreadable.

—Oscar Wilde, "The Decay of Lying"

great poet, a really great poet, is the most unpoetical of creatures. But inferior poets are absolutely fascinating. The worse their rhymes the more picturesque they look. The mere fact of having published a book of second-rate sonnets makes a man quite irresistible. He lives the poetry he cannot write. The others write the poetry that they dare not realise.

—Oscar Wilde, *The Picture of Dorian Gray*

♣

He [James Joyce] died in Zurich early this year, having in the time between reviled the religion in which he had been brought up and fouled the nest which was his native city.

—*The Irish Independent*

Zola is determined to show that, if he has not got genius, he can at least be dull. And how well he succeeds!

—Oscar Wilde

♣

On his cousin, Edward Martyn:
That fellow has no feelings. He quite genuinely believes that I'm damned and he's not even sorry for me!

—George Moore

One man's poetry is another man's poison.

—Oscar Wilde

Bernard Shaw is an excellent man; he has not an enemy in the world, and none of his friends like him.

—Oscar Wilde

George Moore sent a copy of his novel on the life of Christ to his friend AE (George Russell). 'You'll like this better than any of my books,' he wrote. AE replied: On the contrary, I like it less than any of your books. Jesus converted the world; your Jesus wouldn't convert an Irish County Council.

Mr. Henry James writes fiction as if it were a painful duty.

—Oscar Wilde

On George Moore, the artist:
Nobody in Ireland has ever seen any of Mr. Moore's paintings except AE to whom he once slyly showed a head, remarking that it had some 'quality.' AE remained silent.

—Susan Mitchell, *George Moore*

On biography:
Every great man nowadays has his disciples, and it is usually Judas who writes his biography.

—Oscar Wilde

🍀

On George Moore's novel, Esther Waters:
He leads his readers to the latrine and locks them in.

—Oscar Wilde

🍀

Shakespeare might have met Rozencrantz and Guildenstern in the white streets of London, or seen the serving-men of rival houses bite their thumbs at each other in the open square; but Hamlet came out of his soul, and Romeo out of his passion.

—Oscar Wilde, "The Critic as Artist"

🍀

Books of poetry by young writers are usually promissory notes that are never met.

—Oscar Wilde

I never travel without my diary. One should always have something sensational to read in the train.

—Oscar Wilde, *The Importance of Being Earnest*

☘

A lecture by Walter Pater at the London Institution was delivered in a quiet, monotonous voice, as if he were reading to himself. When he enquired of a few friends, 'I hope you all heard me?' Oscar Wilde replied for the others:

We overheard you.

☘

Frank Harris used to boast of his social successes, and of all the grand houses he had stayed at. Oscar Wilde, who had reached the limit of boredom, once cut in:

Yes, dear Frank, we believe you—you have dined in every house in London, once.

Oscar Wilde told the actor Benoît-Constant Coquelin that the play he was writing, The Duchess of Padua, *consisted solely of style, and added:* Between them, Hugo and Shakespeare have exhausted every subject. Originality is no longer possible, even in sin. So there are no real emotions left—only extraordinary adjectives.

♣

A true artist takes no notice whatever of the public. The public to him are non-existent. He leaves that to the popular novelist.

—Oscar Wilde, "The Soul of Man Under Socialism"

George Moore wrote brilliant English until he discovered grammar.

—Oscar Wilde

The only real people are the people who never existed and if a novelist is base enough to go to life for his personages he should at least pretend that they are creations and not boast of them as copies.

—Oscar Wilde, "The Decay of Lying"

When a man acts he is a puppet. When he describes he is a poet.

—Oscar Wilde

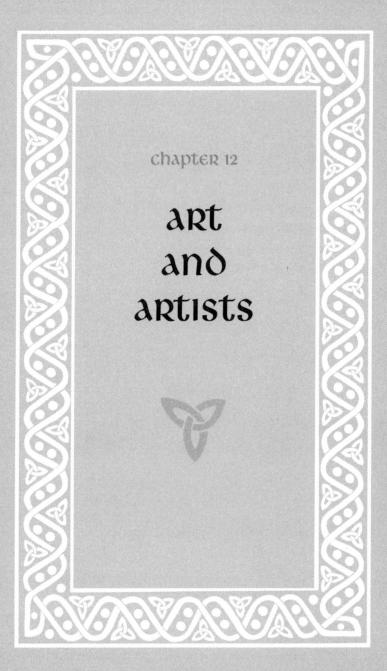

chapter 12

art
and
artists

The discovery of America was the beginning of the death of art.

—Oscar Wilde

♣

Musical people are so absurdly unreasonable. They always want one to be perfectly dumb at the very moment when one is longing to be absolutely deaf.

—Oscar Wilde, *An Ideal Husband*

Artists, like Gods, must never leave their pedestals.

—Oscar Wilde

Venus de Milo was the earliest example of a 'hands-off' policy.

—*The Irish News*

So infinitesimal did I find the knowledge of Art, west of the Rocky Mountains, that an art patron—one who in his day had been a miner—actually sued the railroad company for damages because the plaster-cast Venus de Milo, which he had imported from Paris, had been delivered minus the arms. And, what is more surprising still, he gained his case and the damages.

—Oscar Wilde

♣

People have a careless way of talking about a 'born liar,' just as they talk about a born poet. Lying and poetry are arts—arts, as Plato saw, not unconnected with each other—and they require the most careful study, the most interested devotion.

—Oscar Wilde, "The Decay of Lying"

♣

It is only an auctioneer who can equally and impartially admire all schools of art.

—Oscar Wilde

J ournalists record only what happens. What does it matter what happens? It is only the abiding things that are interesting, not the horrid incidents of everyday life. Creation for the joy of creation is the aim of the artist, and that is why the artist is a more divine type than the saint.

—Oscar Wilde

♣

I like Wagner's music better than anybody's. It is so loud that one can talk the whole time without people hearing what one says.

—Oscar Wilde, *The Picture of Dorian Gray*

♣

The past is of no importance. The present is of no importance. It is with the future that we have to deal. For the past is what man should not have been. The present is what man ought not to be. The future is what artists are.

—Oscar Wilde, "The Soul of Man Under Socialism"

English actors act quite well but they act best
between the lines.

—Oscar Wilde

In the Rockies I saw the only rational method of
art criticism I have ever come across. Over the
piano was printed a notice: 'Please do not shoot the
pianist: he is doing his best.' The mortality among
pianists in that place is marvellous.

—Oscar Wilde

I love acting. It is so much more real than life.

—Oscar Wilde, *The Picture of Dorian Gray*

No work of art ever puts forward views. Views
belong to people who are not artists.

—Oscar Wilde

The only artists I have ever known who are personally delightful are bad artists. Good artists exist simply in what they make and consequently are perfectly uninteresting in what they are.

—Oscar Wilde, *The Picture of Dorian Gray*

Nature is elbowing her way into the charmed circle of Art.

—Oscar Wilde

At present the newspapers are trying hard to induce the public to judge a sculptor, for instance, never by his statues but by the way he treats his wife; a painter by the amount of his income; and a poet by the colour of his necktie.

—Oscar Wilde

I am always amused by the silly vanity of those writers and artists of our day who seem to imagine that the primary function of the critic is to chatter about their second-rate work.

—Oscar Wilde, "The Critic as Artist"

♣

People sometimes enquire what form of government it is most suitable for an artist to live under. To this question there is only one answer. The form of government that is most suitable to the artist is no government at all.

—Oscar Wilde, "The Soul of Man Under Socialism"

♣

In San Francisco Oscar Wilde told his listeners that pictures ought to be hung on the eye-line:
The habit in America of hanging them up near the cornice struck me as irrational at first. It was not until I saw how bad the pictures were that I realised the advantage of the custom.

When the public say a work is grossly unintelligible, they mean that the artist has said or made a beautiful thing that is new. When they describe a work as grossly immoral, they mean that the artist has said or made a beautiful thing that is true.

—Oscar Wilde, "The Soul of Man Under Socialism"

To reveal art and conceal the artist is art's aim.

—Oscar Wilde, *The Picture of Dorian Gray*

There is hardly a single person in the House of Commons worth painting, though many of them would be the better for a little whitewashing.

—Oscar Wilde

Most of our modern portrait painters are doomed to oblivion. They never paint what they see. They paint what the public sees, and the public never sees anything.

—Oscar Wilde, "The Decay of Living"

The only portraits in which one believes are portraits where there is very little of the sitter and a very great deal of the artist.

—Oscar Wilde, "The Decay of Lying"

No great artist ever sees things as they really are. If he did he would cease to be an artist.

—Oscar Wilde, "The Decay of Lying"

Exasperated musician to pupil: 'Really, I can't believe that you were born with even drums in your ears.'

—*Cork Examiner*

One should either be a work of art, or wear a work of art.

—Oscar Wilde, "Phrases and Philosophies
for the Use of the Young"

She is like most artists; she is all style without any sincerity.

—Oscar Wilde, "The Nightingale and the Rose"

It is only an auctioneer who can equally and impartially admire all schools of art.

—Oscar Wilde, "The Critic as Artist"

The telling of beautiful untrue things is the proper aim of art.

—Oscar Wilde, "The Decay of Lying"

All art is at once surface and symbol. Those who go beneath the surface do so at their peril. Those who read the symbol do so at their peril.

—Oscar Wilde, *The Picture of Dorian Gray*

nobody of any real culture ever talks about the beauty of a sunset. Sunsets are quite old-fashioned. They belong to the time when Turner was the last note in art. To admire them is a distinct sign of provincialism. Upon the other hand they go on. Yesterday evening Mrs. Arundel insisted on my going to the window and looking at the glorious sky, as she called it. Of course I had to look at it. She is one of those absurdly pretty Philistines to whom one can deny nothing. And what was it? It was simply a very second-rate Turner, a Turner of bad period, with all the painter's worst faults exaggerated and over-emphasised.

—Oscar Wilde, "The Decay of Lying"

♣

When they stood up to sing, there was not an empty seat in the whole sacred building.

—*Newry Telegraph*

♣

The proper school to learn art is not Life but Art.

—Oscar Wilde, "The Decay of Lying"

A really well-made buttonhole is the only link
between Art and Nature.

—Oscar Wilde, "Phrases and Philosophies
for the Use of the Young"

Music makes one feel so romantic—at least it
always got on one's nerves—which is the same
thing nowadays.

—Oscar Wilde, *A Woman of No Importance*

We can forgive a man for making a useful thing
as long as he does not admire it. The only excuse
for making a useless thing is that one admires it
intensely. All art is quite useless.

—Oscar Wilde, *The Picture of Dorian Gray*

Art is the most intense mode of individualism that
the world has known.

—Oscar Wilde, "The Soul of Man Under Socialism"

The best that one can say of most modern creative
art is that it is just a little less vulgar than reality.

—Oscar Wilde, "The Critic as Artist"

It is not good
for one's morals
to see bad acting.

—Oscar Wilde, *The Picture of Dorian Gray*

All art is immoral. For emotion for the sake of
emotion is the aim of art, and emotion for the sake
of action is the aim of life.

—Oscar Wilde, "The Critic as Artist"

♣

If one plays good music people don't listen, and if
one plays bad music people don't talk.

—Oscar Wilde, *The Importance of Being Earnest*

Nature is always behind the age. It takes a great artist to be thoroughly modern.

—Oscar Wilde

On seeing the painter William Powell Frith's The Derby Day, *which was bought for England:*
Is it really all done by hand?

—Oscar Wilde

♣

That curious mixture of bad painting and good intentions that always entitles a man to be called a representative British artist.

—Oscar Wilde

It is the spectator, and not life, that art really mirrors.

—Oscar Wilde, *The Picture of Dorian Gray*

modern pictures are, no doubt, delightful to look at. At least, some of them are. But they are quite impossible to live with; they are too clever, too assertive, too intellectual. Their meaning is too obvious, and their method too clearly defined. One exhausts what they have to say in a very short time, and then they become as tedious as one's relations.

—Oscar Wilde, "The Critic as Artist"

♣

Art is rarely intelligible to the criminal classes.

—Oscar Wilde

♣

The first duty of an art critic is to hold his tongue at all times, and upon all subjects.

—Oscar Wilde, "The English Renaissance of Art"

chapter 13

life
and
living

Every impulse that we strive to strangle broods in the mind and poisons us…The only way to get rid of temptation is to yield to it.

—Oscar Wilde

♣

To get into the best society nowadays, one has either to feed people, amuse people, or shock people—that is all.

—Oscar Wilde

♣

A famous landlord was renowned for late rising, usually taking his breakfast when the rest of the family were having lunch. Asked one day to account for his habit he replied:
The fact is I sleep very slowly.

♣

The value of the telephone is the value of what two people have to say.

—Oscar Wilde

Very few men, properly speaking, live at present, but are providing to live another time.

—Dean Jonathan Swift

Memory is the diary that we all carry about with us.

—Oscar Wilde, *The Importance of Being Earnest*

No civilised man ever regrets a pleasure, and no uncivilised man ever knows what a pleasure is.

—Oscar Wilde, *The Picture of Dorian Gray*

Nothing can cure the soul but the senses, just as nothing can cure the senses but the soul.

—Oscar Wilde, *The Picture of Dorian Gray*

A man had been trying for a job but was continually being turned down at the local factory. One day in exasperation he said:
When you have plenty of work you give it to others; when you have none you give it to me.

🍀

Half the lies our opponents tell about us are not true.

—Sir Boyle Roche

🍀

To have been well brought up is a great drawback nowadays. It shuts one out from so much.

—Oscar Wilde, *A Woman of No Importance*

OVERHEARD IN DUBLIN

"The last time the fortune teller told her that she'd be very unhappy until she was forty but that after that she'd get used to it."

An Irish chiropodist's announcement:
I have extracted corns from all the crowned heads of Europe.

❧

There is a good deal to be said for blushing, if one can do it at the proper moment.

—Oscar Wilde, *A Woman of No Importance*

❧

If you don't get up and go downtown you'd hear nothing, nor find what they're saying about you. And God send they're saying something. Good or bad, it's better to be criticised than ignored.

—Brendan Behan

❧

In her dealings with man Destiny never closes her accounts.

—Oscar Wilde, *The Picture of Dorian Gray*

To live is the rarest thing in the world. Most people exist, that is all.

—Oscar Wilde, "The Soul of Man Under Socialism"

Those who see any difference between soul and body have neither.

—Oscar Wilde, "Phrases and Philosophies
for the Use of the Young"

Tyranny is worse than a crime—it is an extravagance.

—Tom Kettle

Discontent is the first step in the progress of a man or a nation.

—Oscar Wilde, *A Woman of No Importance*

The first duty of life is to be as artificial as possible; what the second duty is, no one has yet discovered.

—Oscar Wilde

🍀

A Lord Mayor of Dublin was giving a farewell supper and during the last speech said:
I am making my debut for the last time.

I can resist everything except temptation.

—Oscar Wilde, *Lady Windermere's Fan*

Life is a cheap *table d'hote* in a rather dirty restaurant, with time changing the plates before you have had enough of anything.

—Tom Kettle

If there was less sympathy in the world there would be less trouble in the world.

—Oscar Wilde, *An Ideal Husband*

To make a good salad, is to be a brilliant diplomatist— the problem is the same in both cases. To know exactly how much oil to put with one's vinegar.

—Oscar Wilde, *Vera, or the Nihilists*

Soil: That from which farmers and laundries make a living.

—*Farmers' Journal*

Duke: Have prudence in your dealings with the world. Be not too hasty; act on the second thought, first impulses are generally good.

—Oscar Wilde, *The Duchess of Padua*

It is pure unadulterated country life. They get up early because they have so much to do and go to bed early because they have so little to think about.

—Oscar Wilde, *The Picture of Dorian Gray*

♣

Seriousness is the only refuge of the shallow!

—Oscar Wilde

♣

Single misfortunes never come alone but the worst of all misfortunes is generally followed by a greater.

—Sir Boyle Roche

♣

Moderation is a fatal thing. Nothing succeeds like excess.

—Oscar Wilde, *A Woman of No Importance*

♣

Laughter: The chorus of conversation.

—Traditional

Vulgarity and stupidity are two very vivid facts in modern life. One regrets them, naturally. But there they are.

—Oscar Wilde, "The Soul of Man Under Socialism"

Experience is the name everyone gives to their mistakes.

—Oscar Wilde, *Lady Windermere's Fan*

Philosophy is a blanket which men have woven to protect themselves from life.

—Tom Kettle

We are each our own devil, and we make this world our hell.

—Oscar Wilde, *The Duchess of Padua*

On sewage smells:
The smells you don't smell are the smells that do you most harm.

—A Waterford council official

Nothing looks
so like innocence
as an indiscretion.

—Oscar Wilde, "Lord Arthur Savile's Crime"

I hope you have not been leading a double life, pretending to be wicked and being really good all the time. That would be hypocrisy.

—Oscar Wilde, *The Importance of Being Earnest*

Nothing makes one so vain as being told that one is a sinner.

—Oscar Wilde, *The Picture of Dorian Gray*

Life would be a nobler thing if we avoided petty tittle-tattle about our neighbours but the evenings would be terribly long.

—Lynn Doyle

Professor Robert Yelverton Tyrrell always raged when he saw a sign saying 'Temperance Hotel'. He would tell the proprietor:
There is no such thing, you might as well talk of a celibate brothel.

I concluded from the beginning that this would be the end of it, and I see I was right, for it is not half over yet.

—Sir Boyle Roche

One should absorb the colour of life, but one should never remember its details. Details are always vulgar.

—Oscar Wilde, *The Picture of Dorian Gray*

Three things a man can never fathom:
A woman's mind.
The work of the bees.
The ebb and flow of the tides.

—Traditional

♣

A truth ceases to be a truth when more than one
person believes in it.

—Oscar Wilde, "Phrases and Philosophies
for the Use of the Young"

OVERHEARD IN DUBLIN

MAN: Missus, will these flowers last a long time,
then?
WOMAN: Ah, isn't that the six-mark question, luv.
Sure if any of us were cut off in our bloom and
then put up to our arse in water would we hold
out very long?

It is better to take pleasure in a rose than to put its root under a microscope.

—Oscar Wilde

The world is a stage, but the play is badly cast.

—Oscar Wilde, "Lord Arthur Savile's Crime"

As a woman rushed with a kettle to pour the water over some burning curtains, her husband shouted at her:
Don't be a fool, Mary, sure that water's no good—
it's boiling.

To believe is very dull. To doubt is intensely engrossing. To be on the alert is to live; to be lulled into security is to die.

—Oscar Wilde

When we are happy we are always good, but when we are good we are not always happy.

—Oscar Wilde, *The Picture of Dorian Gray*

It is with ideas, as with umbrellas; if left lying about they are peculiarly liable to a change of ownership.

—Tom Kettle

Mr. Speaker, how could I be in two places at once unless I were a bird.

—Sir Boyle Roche

♣

I usually say what I really think. A great mistake nowadays. It makes one so liable to be misunderstood.

—Oscar Wilde

Find expression for a sorrow, and it will become dear to you. Find expression for a joy, and you intensify its ecstasy.

—Oscar Wilde, "The Critic as Artist"

Always behave like a duck—keep calm and un-ruffled on the surface, but paddle like the devil underneath.

—Lord Brabazon of Tara

We live in an age that reads too much to be wise, and thinks too much to be beautiful.

—Oscar Wilde, *The Picture of Dorian Gray*

Conscience and cowardice are really the same things. Conscience is the trade-name of the firm.

—Oscar Wilde, *The Picture of Dorian Gray*

The one duty we owe to history is to rewrite it.

—Oscar Wilde, "The Critic as Artist"

I place great faith in my own anonymity. It's only if you go to the office so that they can see what they've hired, that you're likely to get the sack.

— Patrick Campbell, *My Life and Easy Times*

No crime is vulgar, but all vulgarity is crime.

—Oscar Wilde, "Phrases and Philosophies for the Use of the Young"

I always pass on good advice. It is the only thing to do with it. It is never any use to oneself.

—Oscar Wilde, *An Ideal Husband*

A good word never broke a tooth.

—Traditional

I hope you don't think you have exhausted life…
When a man says that, one knows that life has
exhausted him.

—Oscar Wilde, *A Woman of No Importance*

Questions are never indiscreet. Answers sometimes are.

—Oscar Wilde, *An Ideal Husband*

Nobody running at full speed has either a head or a heart.

—William Butler Yeats

Life is much too important a thing ever to talk
seriously about it.

—Oscar Wilde, *Vera, or the Nihilists*

I never approve, or disapprove, of anything now. It is an absurd attitude to take towards life. We are not sent into the world to air our moral prejudices. I never take any notice of what common people say, and I never interfere with what charming people do.

—Oscar Wilde, *The Picture of Dorian Gray*

Society often forgives the criminal; it never forgives the dreamer.

—Oscar Wilde, "The Critic as Artist"

Life: A lament in one ear and a song in the other.

—Sean O'Casey

Moods don't last. It is their chief charm.

—Oscar Wilde, *A Woman of No Importance*

OVERHEARD IN DUBLIN

WOMAN #1: Well, Theresa, will ye get your stockin' filled this Christmas?

WOMAN #2: Oh, I will, luv, with me bleedin' leg.

Life…is simply a *mauvais quart d'heure* made up of exquisite moments.

—Oscar Wilde, *A Woman of No Importance*

We can have in life but one great experience at best, and the secret of life is to reproduce that experiece as often as possible.

—Oscar Wilde, *The Picture of Dorian Gray*

All along the untrodden paths of the future I can see the footprints of an unseen hand.

—Sir Boyle Roche

The world has been made by fools that wise men should live in it.

—Oscar Wilde, *A Woman of No Importance*

♣

A watched pot never boils.

—Traditional

♣

It is always a silly thing to give advice, but to give good advice is absolutely fatal.

—Oscar Wilde

♣

Success: The only infallible criterion of wisdom to vulgar judgment.

—Edmund Burke

♣

It is because Humanity has never known where it was going that it has been able to find its way.

—Oscar Wilde, "The Critic as Artist"

I wrote when I did not know life; now that I do know the meaning of life, I have no more to write. Life cannot be written; life can only be lived.

—Oscar Wilde

Never put your hand out further than you can draw it back again.

—Traditional

Letter from a Dublin firm:
We beg to inform you that all vacancies are full.

What people call insincerity is simply a method by which we can multiply our personalities.

—Oscar Wilde

overheard in dublin

"I'm telling ye, luv, what I had to go through this morning, half of them undecided as to what they wanted and the other half who couldn't make up their minds. I'm telling ye, if Christ was working down here he'd ask to be crucified quick."

Society produces rogues, and education makes one rogue cleverer than another.

—Oscar Wilde

🍀

I adore simple pleasures; they are the last refuge of the complex.

—Oscar Wilde, *A Woman of No Importance*

🍀

To know everything about oneself one must know all about others.

—Oscar Wilde

To his shoemaker:
Oh! you're a precious blockhead to do directly the
reverse of what I desired you. I told you to make
one of the shoes larger than the other, and instead
of that you have made one of them smaller than
the other.

—Sir Boyle Roche

One who lies down
with dogs will get up
with fleas.

—Traditional

People should not mistake the means of civilisation
for the end. The steam engine and the telephone
depend entirely for their value on the use to which
they are put.

—Oscar Wilde

If you pretend to be good, the world takes you very seriously. If you pretend to be bad, it doesn't. Such is the astounding stupidity of optimism.

—Oscar Wilde, *Lady Windermere's Fan*

To be natural is such a very difficult pose to keep up.

—Oscar Wilde, *An Ideal Husband*

If one tells the truth, one is sure, sooner or later, to be found out.

—Oscar Wilde, "Phrases and Philosophies for the Use of the Young"

In this world there are only two tragedies. One is not getting what one wants and the other is getting it.

—Oscar Wilde, *Lady Windermere's Fan*

What seem to us bitter trials are often blessings in disguise.

—Oscar Wilde, *The Importance of Being Earnest*

I answer in the affirmative with an emphatic 'No.'

—Sir Boyle Roche

At a public dinner it is not so much the menu that matters as the man you sit next to.

—Tom Kettle

If a man treats life artistically, his brain is in his heart.

—Oscar Wilde, *The Picture of Dorian Gray*

It is always nice to be expected and not to arrive.

—Oscar Wilde, *An Ideal Husband*

chapter 14

sports
and
hobbies

Antique: Something no one would be seen with if there were more of them, but which everyone wants when no one has any.

—Traditional

♣

During a competition at Hermitage Golf Club a few years ago the secretary saw a competitor about to drive off a few yards in front of the tee box. 'You must not do that' he said. 'Mind your own business,' said the member. 'I'll have you know I'm the secretary here and it is my job to see that the competition rules are observed. If you hit that ball you are disqualified.' The member ceased addressing the ball and turned bitterly on the secretary: Again I tell you to mind your own business. I'm playing my third.

♣

The curse of it is that when you're learning golf you hit nothing and when you're learning motoring you hit everything.

—*Dublin Opinion*

On the three games of football common to Ireland:
In rugby you kick the ball, in soccer you kick the man if you cannot kick the ball, in Gaelic you kick the ball if you cannot kick the man.

—Anonymous

♣

On Ronnie Delany's achievement in the 1956 Olympic Games:
He was so fast, that everyone else in the race had to run twice as fast to keep up with him.

—Anonymous

Cultivated leisure is the aim of man.

—Oscar Wilde, "The Soul of Man Under Socialism"

The horse: A friend of man so long as man doesn't bet on him.

—*Dublin Opinion*

*One fine morning the Kildare hounds had brought
their fox to bay and were killing it on the far side of a
stream, too wide to jump and too deep to ride through.
The Master was anxious to find out if his hounds were
on a dogfox or a vixen, so he shouted across to a man
standing on the far side: 'Is it a vixen, is it a vixen?'
The man made no reply. The Master shouted again still
louder: 'Is it a vixen?' The man shouted back:*
How the hell should I know? Sure the dogs have
eaten all the sex out of it.

🍀

On poker:
Like most of the distinctly national products of
America, and seems to have been imported from
abroad.

—Oscar Wilde

🍀

*Asked how many his jaunting car would hold the
Killarney man replied:*
If you sit contagious it will hold four and if you sit
familiar it will hold six.

Irate huntsman (to new groom): Look here, confound you! I won't have this! Do you think I'm a fool? Groom: Sure, sir, I can't say, sir. I only came here yesterday!

♣

A Galway farmer had just bought a very poor looking horse from a tinker.
Wife: How much did you give for him?
Farmer: I gave four pound for him.
Wife: You don't tell me! Well you couldn't have got a better one for less.

♣

One knows so well the popular idea of health. The English country gentleman galloping after a fox— the unspeakable in full pursuit of the uneatable.

—Oscar Wilde, *A Woman of No Importance*

♣

One should always play fairly—when one has the winning cards.

—Oscar Wilde, *An Ideal Husband*

Brendan Behan was a great man for swimming—and he wasn't always worried about the convention of dressing. Once on a crowded beach he ran to the water without a stitch on, roaring as he went:
Close your eyes, girls, I'm coming through.

> # I do not play cricket because it requires me to assume such indecent postures.
>
> —Oscar Wilde

A man was buying a horse from a tinker at Ballinasloe Fair:
Buyer: Is this a good horse that you're selling me?
Seller: For what do you want him?
Buyer: For sending to England.
Seller: Oh he'll do well for that; he's a good horse for exportation; he's very well at sea if he isn't worth much upon land.

Hobby: Hard work that you would be ashamed to do for a living.

—Traditional

I feel that football is all very well as a game for rough girls, but it is hardly suitable for delicate boys.

—Oscar Wilde

An Irish horse-dealer is said to have sold a mare as sound in wind and limb and 'without fault'. It afterwards appeared that the poor beast could not see at all out of one eye, and was almost blind in the other. The purchaser, finding this, made heavy complaints to the dealer and reminded him that he engaged the mare to be 'without fault'. The dealer replied:

To be sure, to be sure I did, but then, my dear, the poor crater's blindness is not her fault, but her misfortune.

justice
and
the law

A lawyer was dining with Jonathan Swift and, hoping to make a joke with the Dean, asked: 'Suppose, doctor, that the parsons and the devil went to law, which, in your opinion, would win the case?' Swift replied:
The devil would. All the lawyers and attorneys would be on his side.

🍀

Starvation, and not sin, is the parent of modern crime.

—Oscar Wilde, "The Soul of Man Under Socialism"

🍀

A blustering Irish barrister once told John Philpot Curran that he would put him in his pocket if he provoked him further. The reply:
If you do so, you will have more law in your pocket than you ever had in your head.

🍀

Verdict of an Irish jury:
We find that the man who stole the mare is not guilty.

With trial by jury I have lived and, thank God, with trial by jury I shall die.

—Sir Boyle Roche

Judge: If you say another word, I'll commit you.
John Philpot Curran: If your lordship shall do so,
we shall both of us have the consolation of reflecting
that I am not the worst thing that your lordship
has committed.

♣

As one reads history…one is absolutely sickened,
not by the crimes that the wicked have committed,
but by the punishments that the good have inflicted;
and a community is infinitely more brutalised by
the habitual employment of punishment than it is
by the occasional occurrences of crime.

—Oscar Wilde

Arguing for the Habeas Corpus Suspension Bill in Ireland:
It would be better, Mr. Speaker, to give up not only
a part, but, if necessary, even the whole of our
Constitution, to preserve the remainder.

—Sir Boyle Roche

Once they abolish hanging in this country they will have to hang twice as many.

—Anonymous

*During an argument with a colleague on corporal
punishment in schools, Professor J.P. Mahaffy was
declaiming against the practice on the grounds that,
when once inflicted, the damage could not be remedied.
'The only time I ever was swished,' said the professor,
'was for telling the truth.' The colleague replied:*
Well, Mahaffy, it was effective in your case, for it
certainly cured you.

A witness, breaking down under the deadly cross-questioning of John Philpot Curran, complained to the judge that the lawyer confused him. Curran remarked:
Yes, a confusion of the head arising from a corruption of the heart.

John Philpot Curran once said that he could never speak for a quarter of an hour in public without moistening his lips. One of his listeners, Sir Thomas Turton, said: 'I have the advantage on you there, Curran, I spoke the other night for five hours in the House of Commons and never felt in the least thirsty.' Curran said:
That is very remarkable indeed for everyone agrees that it was the driest speech of the session.

A Cork man appeared on a very serious charge and was not represented by counsel. 'You know this is a most serious case,' said the judge, 'are you sure you have no counsel?' He replied:

I'm sure, your honour. I have no counsel but you'll be glad to hear that I have some very good friends on the jury.

❧

A lawyer was challenging a doctor's evidence:

Lawyer: Doctors sometimes make mistakes.

Doctor: The same as lawyers.

Lawyer: But doctors' mistakes are buried six foot under.

Doctor: Yes, and lawyers' mistakes sometimes swing in the air.

❧

John Parsons was travelling with the merciless Lord Norbury, known as the Hanging Judge when they passed a gibbet:

Norbury: Where would you be now if that gallows had its due?

Parsons: Riding alone, my lord.

*'Do you see anything ridiculous in my wig?' asked a
vain barrister whose displaced wig had caused some
merriment in court. John Philpot Curran answered:*
Nothing, except your head.

♣

*A man charged in Clare court with stealing a hay fork
was told that the prosecution could produce two wit-
nesses who saw him do it. He replied:*
Well, I can find a dozen who didn't.

♣

Judge: The case is proved, we award your wife £1
a week.
Husband: That's very kind of your honour, I'll try
and give her a few bob meself.

♣

*A judge insisted on holding a court in a small Irish
town on Good Friday despite objections. Commented
a lawyer:*
Well, your lordship, you'll be the first judge to sit
on this day since Pontius Pilate.

A Carlow man charged with assault was asked whether he was guilty or not. He answered:
How can I tell your honour, till I have heard the evidence?

🍀

John Philpot Curran, once engaged in legal argument, noticed that behind him stood a barrister, tall and thin, who had originally intended taking Holy Orders. The case was about a question of ecclesiastical law:
John Philpot Curran: I should refer your Worship to a high authority behind me, who was intended for the church, though in my opinion he was fitter for the steeple.

🍀

A court case about a fatal dose of poison given to a horse:
Lord Morris: The twelve grains you gave, wouldn't that kill the devil himself if he swallowed it?
Doctor: I don't know, my lord, I have never prescribed for him.
Lord Marsh: Ah, no, doctor, indeed you haven't—the ould boy is still alive.

On guarding the Shannon:
Sir, I would anchor a frigate off each bank of the river, with strict orders not to stir; and so, by cruising up and down, put a stop to smuggling.

—Sir Boyle Roche

♣

To judge, when asked if he knew where he was:
I'm in court where you dispense with justice.

—Witness

♣

The District Justice, looking at the bulky manuscript in a witness's hand, remarked: 'Could you not give us the gist of it?' To which the witness replied:
It's all gist, your honour.

♣

'Hanging Judge' Norbury was asked at a Bar dinner one day if he would care for some beef:
Norbury: Is it hung?
John Philpot Curran: Oh, you have only to try it, and it is sure to be hung!

*Judge Fitzgibbon (later Lord Chancellor Clare) in a
discussion with John Philpot Curran in court one day
exclaimed rather sharply in reply to some legal point
urged by Curran, 'Oh, if that he the law, Mr. Curran,
I may burn my law books!' Curran replied:*
You had better read them, my lord.

*Digby Seymour was carrying on a conversation during
the hearing of a case:*
Judge: Please Mr. Saymour, be quiet.
Digby Seymour: My name is not Saymour, it is
Seymour.
Judge: Well, sir, see more and say less.

*While John Philpot Curran was addressing Lord
Chancellor Clare in a most important case, the judge
occupied himself with giving too much attention to a
favourite Newfoundland dog seated by him in court.
When Curran, having ceased speaking through indig-
nation, Lord Clare raised his head, and asked: 'Why
don't you proceed, Mr. Curran?' Curran responded:*
I thought your Lordships were in consultation.

The foreman of an Irish jury returned to say:
They could not reach a verdict as he had eleven stubborn brutes to deal with.

F. E. Smith (later Lord Birkenhead) was cross-examining a nervous little Irishman in the witness-box:
Smith: Have you ever been married?
Witness: Yes, sir. Once.
Smith: Whom did you marry?
Witness: A, er, a woman, sir.
Smith: Of course, of course. Did you ever hear of anyone marrying a man?
Witness: Yes, sir—my sister did.

A well-known District Justice was sitting in the lounge of a hotel on a hot day drinking a steaming cup of coffee. A close friend arrived and sat down:
Friend: Why don't you drink something cooling? Have you ever tried chilled gin and tonic?
District Justice: No, but I've tried a lot of fellows who have.

To one unfortunate sentenced to hang for stealing a watch:
Aha, you rascal, you reached for time but grasped eternity!

—Judge Norbury

All ye blackguards
who aren't lawyers
leave the court.

—Irish court crier

Describing a witness:
She had all the characteristics of a poker except its occasional warmth.

—Daniel O'Connell

♣

A friend who asked Daniel O'Connell for his autograph got this handwritten reply:
Sir, I never send autographs, Yours, Daniel O'Connell.

Judge: Have you anyone in court who can vouch for your reputation?

Accused: Indeed I have, your honour, the Chief Constable.

Chief Constable: I don't know this man!

Accused: There you are, sir, I've lived in the same district as the Chief Constable for twenty years and he doesn't even know me...isn't that recommendation enough?

♣

Policeman reprimanding an impulsive pedestrian:
Whenever you see a policeman standing in the middle of the street doing nothing he is directing the traffic.

♣

On meeting a friend who was sporting a large pair of whiskers:
Daniel O'Conell: When do you intend to place your whiskers on the peace establishment?

Friend: When you put your tongue on the civil list.

Judge Peter O'Brien was regarded as one of the
gay sparks of the bench and a pretty witness could
often turn the case before him. On one occasion,
barrister Paddy Kelly was endeavouring to bolster
a weak case by reading the most romantic parts
of the correspondence. After a while Peter lifted
a deprecating hand and lisped with a melancholy
smile:

Mithter Kelly, Mithter Kelly, it won't do; it won't
do at all. There wath a time when thuch thingth
interethed me; but I regret to thay I am an exthinct
volcano!

Kelly: Begor, me Lord, I think there's a r-rumble in
the old crater yet!

—Maurice Healy, KC, *The Old Munster Circuit*

In a cross-examination of a witness in a case where the
illegal sale of drink was the charge:
Lawyer said: Did you give him drink from the
motorcar?
Witness: I did not.
Lawyer: Did you give him drink from a glass then?
Witness: I did.

District Justice: Who is appearing for you, my man?
Old farmer: I'm appearin' for myself, sir.
District Justice: Are you pleading guilty or not guilty?
Old farmer: I'm innocent, sir. Sure, if I was guilty
I'd have a lawyer.

♣

Woman: Could you direct me to an honest lawyer?
Daniel O'Connell: Well now, ma'am, that beats me
entirely.

chapter 16

the
hard
stuff

A priest to a bride holding up a sozzled groom at the altar: 'Take him away and bring him back when he's sober.' The bride responded:
But please, your reverence, when he's sober he won't come.

♣

The temperance advocate from Belfast was about to address a gathering in an Orange Hall in County Down. Suddenly there was a lot of tittering among the audience. The speaker, on looking behind, found that he had placed his two posters, 'Alcohol is Poison' and 'Water is Best,' immediately beside a slogan of the local Orangemen that read:
In Union is Strength.

♣

There is a story told of Bishop Healy of Galway once going to the local barber for a shave. Unfortunately the barber was recovering from one of his drunken bouts and nicked the Bishop's face badly.
Bishop: Oh! This cursed drinking!
Barber: Yes, it leaves the skin awful tender.

overheard in dublin

WOMAN #1: Well, there was I in the pub, and over he comes and says that he wouldn't insult me by offerin' me a drink.

WOMAN #2: And what did ye say to that?

WOMAN #1: Oh, says I, I was always one to swally an insult.

Sir Edward Carson: Were you intoxicated?
Defendant: That's my business.
Carson: Have you any other business?

A final toast at a function before the chairman closed it:

Mr. Chairman and gentlemen, the toast that I have the honour to submit is that of Absent Friends and with that toast I would like to couple the name of the wine waiter who was supposed to look after me tonight.

—Jacques McCarthy

The renowned Dr. Mouillot received a hurried call from a farmer who lived in a Wexford town. He found him suffering from a severe case of pneumonia. 'What have you been doing with yourself at all?' he asked the patient. The farmer answered:

Nothing at all, doctor. Yesterday I went to the fair at Ferns and when it was over I walked home. When I reached the house I took off my hat and trousers and hung them on the back of the door and went to bed, but, begob, when I woke up in the morning I was lying in a wet ditch and my trousers were hanging from a branch of a tree.

> Oh, [my brother] often takes an alcoholiday.
>
> —Oscar Wilde

Lady Collector: I'm collecting for the drunkards' home.

Mrs. Casey: Then come round about ten o'clock and collect Casey.

Customer: I'll have an Irish cocktail, please.
Bartender: What's that?
Customer: It's half a whiskey with another half added.

🍀

John B. Keane's young son, Bill: Don't drink anymore.
Brendan Behan: Whatever you say, Bill, but I'll just
have one more to wash the last one down.

🍀

*The local priest seeing a parishioner staggering home
drunk commented, 'Ah, Jamesy, I'm afraid you'll find
the road you're going longer than you think.' The
parishioner answered:*
Sure, Father, it's not the length of the road that
worries me but the breadth of it.

🍀

An Irishman's toast to an Englishman:
Here's to you as good as you are; and here's to me as
bad as I am. But as good as you are and as bad as I
am, I am as good as you are as bad as I am.

Sheridan: Now, gentlemen, are we to drink like men or beasts?

Dinner guests: Like men.

Sheridan: Right, let's get drunk; beasts always know when they've had enough.

☘

Dean Jonathan Swift was once accosted by a drunken weaver:

Weaver: I've been spinning it.

Swift: Aye, and reeling it home.

☘

There was the old club man in St. Stephen's Green who always drank his whiskey with his eyes closed. Asked to explain his strange habit he said:

It's like this, whenever I see a glass of whiskey my mouth waters and I don't care to dilute it.

Arriving around midnight at a pub in Newmarket-on-Fergus a surprised visitor found the place still doing a great trade. 'When do you close?' he asked the publican. The answer:

I would say about the middle of November.

Alcohol: A liquid for preserving almost everything but secrets.

—*The Pioneer*

Mr. Asquith was like a drunken man walking along a straight line—the further he went the sooner he fell.

—Sir Edward Carson

♣

Brendan Behan used to say that he only took a drink twice a day—when he was thirsty and when he wasn't.

*The Dublin woman to the doctor after he had
pronounced the cause of her husband's illness:*
How could he have water on the brain when
he hasn't touched a drop for forty years.

♣

*In Limerick there lived two poets: Sean O'Toumy and
Andrew McGrath—the Merry Pedlar. They fought
many battles of wit and verse. O'Toumy once advertised
himself in the following lines which are a translation of
the Irish he used:*
I sell the best brandy and sherry
To make my good customers merry
But at times their finances run short, as it chances
And then I feel very sad, very.

To this McGrath replied:
O'Toumy you boast yourself handy
At selling good ale and bright brandy
But the fact is your liquor
Makes everyone sicker
I tell you that, I, your friend, Andy.

Justice: Do you mean to say that you only had one whiskey?

Defendant: I do, sir.

Justice: And where did you get that one?

Defendant: Oh, at a devil of a lot of places.

♣

A drunk staggered into Bangor churchyard in County Doivn, and fell asleep among the tombstones. Early next morning, a local factory hooter sounded. The drunk woke up, rubbed his eyes, and seeing where he was concluded, not unnaturally, that he had heard Gabriel's Trumpet:

Boys-oh-boys! Not a soul risen but me. This speaks bad for Bangor!

♣

Drunk: When a man feels sophisticated but can't pronounce it.

—The Pioneer

Employer: Michael, you are looking very rocky this morning.

Deliveryman: Yes, sir, I've a bad headache. I was at a christening last night, sir, an' the kid was the only one in the crowd that took water.

♣

A prisoner in a Dublin court to the justice:
I was sober enough to know I was drunk.

OVERHEARD IN DUBLIN

WOMAN #1: Oh, yer man's a hard drinker, luv.
WOMAN #2: Well, I'm surprised to hear that, luv, because after all this time, I'd have thought he'd have found it easy.

chapter 17

food

On dining expensively in Paris:
It's a duty we owe to the dignity of letters.

—Oscar Wilde

♣

Robert Gibbings, a mountain of a man, was once accosted by a tiny Cork woman who looked up from navel height and said:
My God, sir, but you make great use of your food.

♣

Samuel Lover: Bring me a hot plate, waiter, the beef is good but the plates are cold.
Waiter: The hot plates haven't come in yet, sir.
Lover: Well bring them in, man.
Waiter: I mean, sir, they are not in season; hot plates come in in October and go out in May.

♣

The British cook is a foolish woman who should be turned for her iniquities into a pillar of salt which she never knows how to use.

—Oscar Wilde

On a tour of Ireland with a small circus:
You could get atin' and drinkin' for tuppence a pint.

—William G. Fay, a founder of the Abbey Theatre

OVERHEARÒ IN ÒUBLIN

SHOPKEEPER #1: Well, I'll tell ye, Bridie, that wan this morning really had me annoyed, fingering the oranges, sniffing the apples and, finally, doesn't she go over and feel a cucumber for ages.
SHOPKEEPER #2: What did ye say to her, luv?
SHOPKEEPER #1: I said, Pardon me, missus, it doesn't get bigger if ye feel it.

Waiter: How will you have your eggs cooked?
Brannigan: Make any difference in the cost?
Waiter: No.
Brannigan: Then cook 'em with a nice slice o' ham, if you plaise.

J.C. Percy once remarked to a waiter in a Galway
hotel that the weather was very unsettled. The waiter
replied:
Indeed it is, sir, the glass is hard set catering for it.

🍀

J.C. Percy thanking a waiter at the Wicklow Hotel
in Dublin for bringing him his lunch in a hurry, said,
'You're an angel'. The waiter responded:
I am indeed, sir, but I fly low.

🍀

When the city folks arrived at the country bungalow
they'd rented for the summer they found it had just one
flaw—there was no refuse collection. So, they bought
a pig to consume the leftovers and the arrangement
worked beautifully all summer. When ready to return
to their city home, they let it be known they had a pig
for sale and a prospective buyer enquired the price.
They told him:
Well, we paid fifty shillings for him, but we've used
him all summer. Would twenty-five shillings be
too much?

Soup kitchens were often used in Dublin during the war. One woman commenting on the standard of the soup available said:
They make it like this: they take a gallon of water and then they boil it down to a pint to make it strong.

Lunch is a poor compliment to breakfast and an insult to dinner.

—Father Healy

The visitor to a country hotel asked the waiter for red-currant jelly to go with his mutton. The waiter answered:
Beg your pardon, sir, the jelly is all gone, but I can get you some beautiful lobster sauce.

At a party, a chicken was put before Oscar Wilde to carve. After several attempts he turned to his wife and said:
Constance, why do you give me these...pedestrians...to eat?

A visitor to Connemara asked a tenant what his farm produced to the acre. The answer:
Well, in the summer it might raise enough to feed a hare but in the winter she would have to run for her life.

chapter 18

Religion

Man: What's the Ascendancy?
Brendan Behan: A Protestant on a horse.

♣

One of the reasons why I consider Mahomet a poor prophet—meaning poor poet—was his deciding to go to the mountain when it refused to come to him. If he had been a good poet he would have walked the other way and the mountain would keep following him forever.

—Patrick Kavanagh

♣

A bishop keeps on saying at the age of eighty what he was told to say when he was a boy of eighteen.

—Oscar Wilde

♣

Lord Howe used to tell of an Irish sailor who prayed every night:
Lord, I never murdered any man and no man murdered me; so God bless all mankind.

An Ulster man bought a boat named Pius the Ninth
*from a Wicklow man. He didn't like the name but
could do nothing about it as it was considered unlucky
to change the name of a boat. His wife was telling a
neighbour about the purchase:*

Wife: I'm not well pleased about it. I don't care for
who it's called after.

Neighbour: And who is that?

Wife: Well I wouldn't like to say.

Neighbour: Is it a Roman saint?

Wife: No, it's worse.

Neighbour: Oh Lord, is it a Fenian?

Wife: No, it's still worse.

Neighbour: Lord help us, it must be the devil.

Wife: No, it's even worse than that!

♣

*A parish priest was due to leave the parish and on his
last Sunday the parishioners came to wish him well.
One lady caught him fervently by the hand:*

You are a great man, Father. We knew nothing
about sin until you came among us.

The only difference between the saint and sinner is that every saint has a past, and every sinner has a future.

—Oscar Wilde, *A Woman of No Importance*

You can preach a better sermon with your life than with your lips.

—Oliver Goldsmith

A sermon is a sorry sauce when you have nothing to eat it with.

—Oscar Wilde, *The Duchess of Padua*

Advertisement in a Belfast newspaper:
Wanted: Man and woman to look after two cows, both Protestant.

A man in the professions can never lose. A lawyer is paid—win or lose. A doctor is paid—kill or cure. A priest is paid—heaven or hell.

—An Irish farmer

OVERHEARD IN DUBLIN

"I can't get me young fella to go to Mass anymore, he says it's dead boring 'cause he knows the ending."

Maurice Healy, KC once asked Ulster lawyer John Bartley to explained the difference between a Calvinistic Presbyterian and an ordinary Presbyterian. Bartley answered:

I'll tell ye. A Calvinistic Prasb'tayrian believes all you Papishes wull be domned because ye're predastined to be domned; but we or'nary Prasb'tayrians b'lieve all you Papishes wull be domned on yer mer'ts!

A priest once explained why he commanded his parishioners to say the full Litany of the Saints and not a 'quick' litany:
I was in the church one Saturday evening, and an old woman who is on the deaf side and 'whispers' rather loudly, was praying from her prayer-book this way: 'All the saints on this first page pray for us…all the saints on the second page, pray for us… all the saints on the third page, pray for us…and from all the things on the fourth page, deliver us, O Lord.'

The sick do not ask if the hand that smoothes their pillow is pure, nor the dying care if the lips that touch their brow have known the kiss of sin.

—Oscar Wilde, *A Woman of No Importance*

On his Bray parishioners:
An ideal crowd—the poor keep all the fasts and the rich keep all the feasts.

—Father Healy

The Protestant rector of Bray: I have been sixty years in the world and I have not yet discovered the difference between a good Catholic and a good Protestant.

Father Healy: You won't be sixty seconds in the next world until you find out.

🍀

An Irish atheist is one who wishes to God he could believe in God.

—J.P. Mahaffy

🍀

Pat Hoey, the entertainer, was asked to give a concert in a Carlow town and suggested a fee of three guineas. The parish priest wrote back saying he thought it was a lot and suggested that Pat should make the journey and they would pay him a guinea and promise 'plenty of diversion.' But Pat was not keen. He wrote back:

Dear Rev Father, I am sorry I cannot agree to your committee's terms and incidentally may I, with the greatest respect, submit that anyone who would go to Ballyhill-Murray for 'divarshun' would go to hell for fresh air.

*A clergyman was anxious to introduce some new
hymn-books to his congregation, so he directed
his assistant to make an announcement to that effect
immediately after his sermon. But it so happened
that the assistant had an announcement of his own to
make, as follows: 'All those who have children they wish
to be baptised, please hand in their names at once.' The
clergyman, who was rather deaf, then arose and said:*
And I wish to say, for the benefit of those who
haven't any, that they may be obtained from me any
day between three and four o'clock. The ordinary
little ones are sixpence and the special ones with
red backs are one shilling each.

When I'm in health
I'm not at all religious.
But when I'm sick
I'm very religious.

—Brendan Behan

*Dr. Salmon, Provost of Trinity College, Dublin, used
to tell how his Catholic cook, on contemplating a
Protestant kitchenmaid enjoying a beef-steak on
Friday, pensively remarked:*
If you are not damned for that, all I can say is I have
got a queer sell!

Missionaries, my dear! Don't you realise that
missionaries are the divinely provided food for
destitute and underfed cannibals? Whenever they
are on the brink of starvation, Heaven in its infinite
mercy sends them a nice plump missionary.

—Oscar Wilde

*A Sister was explaining to her class the joys and
wonders of heaven. After several convincing
minutes she asked how many wanted to go to heaven.
All but one little girl raised their hands.*
Sister: Mary, don't you want to go to heaven?
Mary: I want to go all right, Sister, but my mother
told me to come right home after school.

The school-visiting priest: With what weapon did David slay the Philistines?
Student: Please, Father, 'twas with the axe of the Apostles!

In our church one afternoon I saw a little boy hurrying down the side aisle. He was clutching something in his fist—a coin, which he dropped into the box. He picked out a votive candle, lighted it, and knelt down. I knelt down, too, about a yard away. He soon noticed me, but at first he kept his eyes fixed on the altar. A few minutes later he leaned over, and in a resentful whisper said: 'You move over. Pray on your own candle.'

—A church member

A Belfast Catholic was asked what was the most pleasant work he had ever done. He replied:
Pulling down a Protestant church and getting paid for it.

a visiting priest, speaking for a delegation: We have all been wondering where you got your brilliant gift of repartee from?

Father Healy: Now that you have inquired, it must have been from my mother—my father was as common as any of you.

> # I would prefer Heaven for climate but Hell for society as all my friends are Protestants.
>
> —Father Healy

The Bishop of a diocese once stepped in when the local parish priest was taken ill. At the end of his Sunday services a deputation went to thank him:

It was good of your Lordship to help us out today. A worse man would have done but we couldn't find him.

OVERHEARD IN DUBLIN

"Them two wanted flowers for the first communion, red carnations one wanted. 'I'm sorry, luv,' says I, 'I've only these white ones left now.'
'Oh, that won't do at all,' says she, 'they have to be red.'
'Well what do you expect me to do, luv,' says I, 'shed me life's blood over them?"

Asked by Arthur Balfour what his religion was, Oscar Wilde replied:
Well, you know, I don't think I have any. I am an Irish Protestant.

You will soon be going about like the converted and the revivalist, warning people against all the sins of which you have grown tired.

—Oscar Wilde, *The Picture of Dorian Gray*

Priest: What is Baptism?
Child: It used to be two-and-sixpence, but my
mother says it's five bob since you came here.

*A former priest of Sandymount in Dublin had a fine
stocked library but would never loan a book from it.
Once a parishioner asked to borrow a book and was
told he could—provided it was read in the priest's
study. The man declined. A few days later the priest
went to the man's house and asked to borrow his garden
roller. The answer:*
Certainly you can, provided you use it in my garden.

*From a letter written home by Sister M. Stanislaus
McCahe of Carrickmacross:*
Sister Mary Oliver wonders how she should
address His Eminence Cardinal Gracias, India's
first cardinal. You see some people pronounce his
name 'Gracious' while others like the Latin word
Gratias. Which, she asks, is correct? We told her to
say Good Gracious when the Cardinal arrives and
Deo Gratias when his Eminence has departed.

A preacher should ask himself: Am I about to preach because I want to say something or because I have something to say?

—Archbishop Whateley

🍀

Canon O'Connor: Why did Nebuchadnezzar eat grass?
Child in Kilternan School: Because it is written, that he that exalted himself shall be a beast.

🍀

Priest: What do you understand by an 'unclean spirit'?
Child: Please Father, a dirty devil!

🍀

Brevity personified are the letters that passed between the Duke of York and the Protestant Bishop of Cork, referring to the ordination of a man named Ponsonby:
Duke: Dear Cork, Ordain Ponsonby—Yours York.
Bishop: Dear York, Ponsonby ordained—Yours Cork.

An old Irishman, just recovered from a severe attack of sickness, chanced to meet his parish priest, who had been summoned during his illness to administer the last rites of the church:

Priest: Ah, James, I see you are out again. We thought you were gone sure. You had a pretty serious time of it.

James: Yes, Father, indeed I did.

Priest: When you were so near death's door, were you not afraid to meet your God, your Maker?

No, indeed, Father. The other fellow worried me more!

♣

The Protestant vicar of Dalkey was showing his church to Father Healy. 'One thing is sure,' said the vicar, 'my church is built on a rock.' Father Healy responded:

Yes, a blasted one.

♣

The Book of Life begins with a man and woman in a garden. It ends with Revelations.

—Oscar Wilde, *A Woman of No Importance*

*A Belfast Protestant family was getting on the train
when the little girl turned and said:*
Goodbye God, we're going to live in Dublin.

♣

*The priest and the minister were constant but silent
travelling companions. Eventually the minister decided
the silence should be broken:*
Minister: Good day, Father. We see each other
often and I feel we ought to get on speaking terms.
After all we're in the same business.
Priest: Indeed, we are. You're doing it your way
and I'm doing it His.

Sin is a thing that writes
itself across a man's face.
It cannot be concealed.

—Oscar Wilde, *The Picture of Dorian Gray*

*Father Healy, when asked what he thought Tim Healy,
the famous politician, would be when an Irish Parliament
was obtained, retorted:*
An old man.

♣

*The priest was making a collection for a new church.
Said the parish Scrooge:*
Put me down for five pounds, Father. And God
knows, if I had it I'd give it to you.

♣

*One day Father Healy was playing cards with some
members of the peerage at the Viceregal Lodge in Dublin, when he took out a handful of coppers. 'Ah, Father,'
said one of the young peers, 'I see you've been robbing
the offertory box!' Father Healy replied:*
How clever of your Lordship to recognise his own
contribution.

chapter 19

politics
and
government

Dear son, I have written to you five times asking you a simple question but I got no reply. What do you think you are? A government department? Father.

—*Dublin Opinion*

There's two classes of boys that need to have good memories—liars and politicians.

—A Derryman

Agitators are a set of interfering, meddling people, who come down to some perfectly contented class of the community and sow the seeds of discontent amongst them. That is the reason why agitators are so absolutely necessary.

—Oscar Wilde, "The Soul of Man Under Socialism"

Election speech:
The poor people always voted for me, and there are more poor today than ever.

—*Limerick Echo*

🍀

Candidate at election meeting: Now friends what do we need to carry this constituency to the biggest majority in the history of Fianna Fail?
Attendees: Another candidate!

🍀

The Cabinet is said to be the youngest in Europe, but I sometimes detect signs of premature senility.

—Sean Dunne, TD

🍀

In an Irish bank bill of the last century there was a clause:
The profits shall be equally divided and the residue go to the governor.

Good kings are the only dangerous enemies that modern democracy has.

—Oscar Wilde, *Vera, or The Nihilists*

On the possible future of the House of Commons:
[Ruffians] would cut us to mince meat and throw our bleeding heads on that table, to stare us in the face.

—Sir Boyle Roche

On an opponent:
Even if he told the truth I wouldn't believe him.

—An Irish politician

🍀

In England a man who can't talk morality twice a week to a large, popular, immoral audience is quite over as a serious politician. There would be nothing left for him as a profession except Botany or the Church.

—Oscar Wilde, *An Ideal Husband*

The Lords Temporal say nothing, the Lords Spiritual have nothing to say, and the House of Commons has nothing to say and says it.

—Oscar Wilde

This country would die if it didn't have a grievance.

—An Irish TD

Someone threw a head of cabbage at an Irish politician while he was making a speech. He paused a second, and said:
Gentlemen, I only ask for your ears, I don't care for your heads!

The ways of Providence are indeed unscrupulous.

—A well-known politician

The machinery of government—the taxpayer on a treadmill.

—*Dublin Opinion*

🍀

To make men Socialists is nothing, but to make Socialism human is a great thing.

—Oscar Wilde

Gentlemen, it seems unanimous that we cannot agree.

—Charles Stewart Parnell

On a report:
A wholly garbled account of what never took place.

—An Irish politician

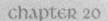

chapter 20

motivation
and
ambition

Ambition is the last refuge of the failure.

—Oscar Wilde, "Phrases and Philosophies
for the Use of the Young"

I never knew any man
who came to greatness
and eminence who lay
in bed in the morning.

—Dean Jonathan Swift

I have no ambition to be a popular hero, to be
crowned with laurels one year and pelted with
stones the next; I prefer dying peaceably in my
own bed.

—Oscar Wilde, *Vera, or The Nihilists*

overheard in dublin

MAN: Look at that, late again this mornin.' Jaysus, that wan would be late for her own funeral.
WOMAN: Oh, it must be her back trouble.
MAN: Yea, I'd say she has great trouble gettin' it off the bed.

The only horrible thing in the world is ennui. That is the one sin for which there is no forgiveness.

—Oscar Wilde

♣

Ambition often puts men upon doing the meanest offices; so climbing is performed in the same posture with creeping.

—Dean Jonathan Swift

Failure: The path of least resistance.

—Traditional

OVERHEARD IN DUBLIN

WOMAN #1: Where's young Jacinta this afternoon luv? Is she not helping ye out?
WOMAN #2: No, luv, it's another of her afternoons off. I'll tell ye something, if she asks for another afternoon off she'll have all her mornings off as well.

When people agree with me I always feel that I must be wrong.

—Oscar Wilde

☘

In a letter to Robert Harborough Sherard:
I am hard at work being idle.

—Oscar Wilde

I must—I will—I can—I ought—I do.

—Richard Brinsley Sheridan

I never put off till tomorrow what I can possibly do the day after.

—Oscar Wilde

On his ambition in life:
God knows! I won't be a dried-up Oxford don, anyhow. I'll be a poet, a writer, a dramatist. Somehow or other I'll be famous, and if not famous I'll be notorious. Or perhaps...I'll rest and do nothing...These things are on the knees of the gods. What will be, will be.

—Oscar Wilde

chapter 21

death
and
dying

The man that was born to be hanged need never fear water.

—Traditional

A few mornings before John Philpot Curran's death a doctor observed to him that he coughed very badly. He said:
That's strange, for I've been practising all night.

An Irishman was explaining to some friends that he thought he saw a ghost one night and took up his gun and shot it. When he got up in the morning he found it was only his shirt. 'What did you do then?' asked his friend. He replied:
I knelt down and thanked God I was not in it.

For Brendan Behan's last quip—looking up at the nun just before he died—he whispered a thank you, and then said:
May you be the mother of a bishop.

Death is not a God. He is only the servant of the Gods.

—Oscar Wilde, *La Sainte Courtisane*

☘

When a man had died and foul play was suspected:
Someone had helped Providence away wi' the crathur.

—*Poor Rabbin's Ollminic*

A thing is not necessarily true because a man dies for it.

—Oscar Wilde, "The Portrait of Mr. W. H."

A barrister friend of J.C. Percy was consulted about a will in which a deceased woman left her house:
...to be sold at my death to provide for my future maintenance.

At the funeral of Lord Longford, Brendan Behan met
a friend of other old hard times, Jimmy Hiney. 'I was
standing at the gate of the Protestant cemetery won-
dering whether I should go in or not,' says Jimmy, 'when
Brendan came up.' Behan said:

Jimmy, I think we'll go in and sing a few hymns for
the ould * * * *. He has as much a chance of heaven
as either of us.

Judge Eugene Sheehy recorded that James Joyce's father
was at breakfast one morning and read an obituary
notice of a dear friend, Mrs. Cassidy:

Mrs. Joyce: Oh! Don't tell me that Mrs. Cassidy
is dead!

Mr. Joyce: Well I don't quite know about that, but
someone has taken the liberty of burying her.

Death and vulgarity are the only two facts in the
nineteenth century that one cannot explain away.

—Oscar Wilde, *The Picture of Dorian Gray*

OVERHEARD IN DUBLIN

MAN: Is Joe around, missus?

WOMAN: No, luv, I'm afraid Joe passed away last week.

MAN: Well, I never, he didn't mention anything about a wheel barra, did he?

The Cavan undertaker was annoyed that a rival had got the job of burying a well-known local personage. As the funeral passed by he said to a friend:
If the man in that coffin was alive I would have his funeral.

♣

An Irishman was opposed to building a new wall around a graveyard because:
Those outside don't want to get in and those inside can't get out.

♣

On a large medical bill:
Ah, well then, I suppose that I shall have to die as I lived—beyond my means.

—Oscar Wilde

♣

She lay at death's door and the doctor pulled her through.

—Anonymous

♣

Father Healy was sinking fast, when he was told that an old friend of his was also dying. He replied:
I'm afraid then that it's going to be a dead heat.

One can survive everything nowadays except death.

—Oscar Wilde

All trials are trials for one's life, and all sentences
are sentences of death.

—Oscar Wilde

If there's music in hell
it'll be the bagpipes.

—Joe Tomelty (Belfast playwright)

On public statues:
To see the frock-coat of the drawing-room done
in bronze, or the double waistcoat perpetuated in
marble, adds a new horror to death.

—Oscar Wilde

♣

*After an oration at the graveside of a famous writer
an old woman was heard to say:*
Wasn't it worth his while to die to have the like
o'that said about him!

nglishman: If the devil was to come here now, which of us do you think he'd take?

Galwayman: He'd take me.

Englishman: Why do you think so?

Galwayman: Because he'd be sure of yourself anytime.

♣

'They say that when good Americans die they go to Paris,' chuckled Sir Thomas...

'Really! And where do bad Americans go to when they die?' inquired the Duchess.

'They go to America,' murmured Lord Henry.

—Oscar Wilde, *The Picture of Dorian Gray*

♣

An undertaker found a donkey lying dead in front of his premises, and went to inform the police:

Undertaker: What'll I do with it?

Police Officer: Do with it? Bury it, of course. You're an undertaker, aren't you?

Undertaker: Certainly I am, but I thought I should come round and inform the relatives first.

Johnny Patterson, the famous Irish clown, lay critically
ill. The doctor, having done all he could, closed his
medicine case and prepared to leave: 'I'll see you in the
morning, Johnny,' he said cheerfully. Instinctively, the
dying clown smirked, gave his eye a professional roll
that had helped launch many a quip, and murmured:
Sure, doc, but will I see you?

I cannot tell you how sorry I was to hear that your
husband has gone to heaven. We were great friends
and it is sad to think that we will never meet again.

—From a letter of condolence to a widow

The Ulsterman had just been told by a clergyman of
the death of an inveterate enemy. 'Well,' he said, 'it's a
comfort to know that the devil's got that fellow at last.'
The clergyman protested against this uncharitable
view, to which the Ulsterman replied:
Well, if the devil hasn't got that fellow, all I can say is
that I don't see much use in us keeping a devil at all.

A man had undergone a rather serious operation in a Dublin nursing home. When he woke up from the anaesthetic he found that although it was broad daylight the blind of his window was fully drawn. He accosted the surgeon who was standing at his bedside. 'Why on earth is the blind drawn?' The surgeon replied: Well, it so happens that the house across the road is on fire; and I was afraid that if you saw it when you woke up you might conclude that the operation had not been a success.

Guide, to visitors, after showing them around the graveyard:
If God spares me, I shall be here myself some day.

Heaven is a despotism; I shall be at home there.

—Oscar Wilde, *Vera, or The Nihilists*

as I was passing a 95 percent female Bingo queue in the city recently, an evening funeral procession approached. I stood in unconcerned respect and as I did so, a middle-aged lady detached herself from the queue. She knelt down upon one knee, and striking her pendulous Dublin bosom three times, murmured 'Mercy, mercy, mercy!' Having rejoined the waiting line her neighbour asked, 'Why did you kneel?' To which she replied: 'Why wouldn't I?—wasn't he a good husband to me?'

—A letter written to the *Irish Times*

There's no
bad publicity
except an obituary.

—Brendan Behan

The Belfast doctor's waiting-room was very full. Every chair was taken and some patients were standing. There was desultory conversation, but after a while a silence fell and the patients sat waiting. Finally, an old man stood up wearily and remarked:

Ach, I think I'll go home and die a natural death.

♣

The farmer looking at the loitering labourer:

You'd be a good messenger to send for death.

♣

On being told he was dying:

Why, dying is the last thing I shall do.

—Lord Palmerston

ABOUT THE CONTRIBUTORS

AE (GEORGE RUSSELL) (1867–1935)
An Irish Nationalist, critic, poet, and painter he was also a mystical writer and one of the major contributors to the Irish Literary Renaissance. Belonging to the Irish Literary Revival, he was responsible for introducing James Joyce to other major Irish literary figures, including William Butler Yeats.

LORD BRABAZON OF TARA (1884–1964)
He was a British Minister and also the first person to be licensed in Great Britain as an Airplane Pilot. In 1909 he made the first live cargo flight by carrying a live pig in a wastepaper basket attached to his plane.

BRENDAN BEHAN (1923–1964)
A devout Irish Republican and volunteer in the Irish Republican Army, Behan was a writer of not only poetry but also short stories, novels, and plays in both English and his native Irish. He spent several years in prison for his IRA activities, which he wrote about in his book *Borstal Boy*.

COUNTESS OF BLESSINGTON (1789–1849)
Novelist and writer, she was propelled into the world of literature after her husband died and she found she could supplement her income writing novels. For several years, she was also the editor of popular annals at the time—*The Book of Beauty* and *The Keepsake*.

EDMUND BURKE (1729–1797)
He served for many years as a member of the Whig party in the British House of Commons. The Anglo-Irish author, orator, political theorist, philosopher and statesman is greatly remembered for his support of the American colonies in the dispute that led to the American Revolution.

FRANKIE BYRNE (1922–1993)
Also know as the 'agony aunt', her legendary radio program was broadcast from 1963-85. With a backdrop of Sinatra albums, she offered volumes of advice for those with romantic problems, becoming a national broadcasting symbol in the 60s and 70s.

PATRICK CAMPBELL (1977–1999)
Originally born in west Belfast, he moved to Dublin for work. Eventually he became a volunteer in the Irish National Liberation Army but met a grisly demise when he was murdered in 1999 by Dublin drug dealers.

SIR EDWARD CARSON (1854–1935)
Considered the 'uncrowned king' of Protestants in Ireland, he was hired by the Marquess of Queensbury to aid in the prosecution of Oscar Wilde, a former classmate at Trinity College. At the time of his death in 1935 he was one of few non-monarchs to receive the esteemed honor of a United Kingdom state funeral.

JOHN COSTELLO (1891–1976)
This barrister was one of the main legal advisors to the government of the Irish Free State. Attorney General of Ireland from 1926–32, he was also a member of the Royal Irish Academy. In March 1975 he was made a Freeman of the city of Dublin.

JOHN PHILPOT CURRAN (1750–1817)
Hailing from Country Cork, he initially tried his hand at being a lawyer. His uncontrollable nerves got the best of him during his first few trials, garnering him the unfortunate nickname 'Stuttering Jack Curran'. Reciting great literary works in front of a mirror enabled him to overcome his nerves and stutter, resulting in his becoming a noted orator of great wit.

DAN DONNELLY (1788–1820)
Born to a carpenter in the 18th century when there were drastic class divisions, Donnelly became the first Irish-born heavyweight champion. Morbidly and respectfully, his mummified right arm has been on display in many an Irish pub.

LYNN DOYLE (1873–1961)
While working as a banker in Dublin, he published the first of thirteen volumes of fiction. He was one of the first writers appointed to the Censorship of Publications Board in 1937, resigning soon afterwards.

St. John Ervine (1883–1971)
He wrote plays utilizing the style of local realism bred from the Irish literary renaissance. After writing his 1956 biography of George Bernard Shaw, he won the James Tait Black Memorial Prize.

Robert Farren (1909–1984)
An Irish poet born into a working-class family, he joined Radio Éireann as Controller of Programmes. His verse plays, which demonstrated Gaelic prosodic patterns, were performed at the Abbey Theatre where he was also director from 1940–73.

Elizabeth Fitzgerald (1527–1589)
This Irish noblewoman was the inspiration for a sonnet written by the Earl of Surrey. She was the wife of Sir Anthony Browne and later of English admiral Edward Clinton, First Earl of Lincoln.

Judge Fitzgibbon (Lord Chancellor Clare) (1749–1802)
After an education at Trinity College he abandoned the Roman Catholic faith to pursue a legal career. He soon acquired a lucrative practice and subsequently inherited his father's vast fortune.

Percy French (1854–1920)
Though he has come to be readily recognized by his watercolor paintings, he was, in his day, one of Ireland's most well known songwriters of the late 19th/early 20th century.

Oliver Goldsmith (1730–1774)
The most notable work by this Anglo-Irish writer, poet, and physician—apart from his numerous plays—is his one and only novel, *The Vicar of Wakefield*. In a time when plays thrived on the dull and sentimental, Goldsmith injected a much needed sense of realism and wit into his comedies.

Maurice Healy (1859–1923)
An Irish nationalist politician, lawyer, and MP in the House of Commons of the United Kingdom of Great Britain and Ireland.

FATHER JAMES HEALY (1824–1894)
The most famous priest of Bray, Father Healy was born in Dublin to a rather sizeable family of twenty-three. His knack for performance and deftly playing on words gave light to the term "Bray wit."

JAMES JOYCE (1882–1941)
Though an Irish expatriate, his written works were deeply rooted in Dublin. His use of experimental language and a mélange of parallels from mythology, history, and literature secured him as one of the most influential writers of the 20th century. He is best known for *Ulysses, Finnegans Wake,* as well the semi-autobiographical novel *A Portrait of the Artist as a Young Man.*

PATRICK KAVANAGH (1904–1967)
His reputation in Ireland came from his stark anti-pastoral poetry and criticism of the church. A self-educated man, he lived in Dublin for the majority of his life as a journalist.

TOM KETTLE (1880–1916)
An Irish writer, journalist, poet, barrister, and economist, he breathed new intellectual life into Irish party politics. He was a gifted speaker of crippling wit and acute intelligence.

SAMUEL LOVER (1797–1868)
An Irish songwriter, novelist, and portrait painter. A number of his songs attained great popularity and he is responsible for creating *Irish Nights*—a combination of his short sketches and songs.

ROBERT LYND (1879–1949)
An Irish writer, his fervent sense of nationalism led him to become a fluent Irish speaker and member of the Gaelic League. He wrote for *The Republic, The Nation,* and *The New Statesman.*

J.P. MAHAFFY (1839–1919)
Regarded doubly as one of Dublin's greatest curmudgeons and greatest wits. With versatility to his intellect, he ranged from being a distinguished authority on Egyptology to a Doctor of Music. His numerous published works on a varied array of topics eventually became standard authorities in their respective categories.

EDWARD MARTYN (1859–1923)

A playwright who was vehemently against British rule of his native Ireland. With friends William Butler Yeats and Lady Gregory he co-founded the Irish Literary Theatre. He died unmarried, and at his request was buried in a pauper's grave.

SUSAN MITCHELL (1866–1926)

Her biting satirical commentary secured her a spot in the cultural renaissance of the early 20th century where she was revered as a poet, editor, and even mystic. Adopted by aunts at an early age she was required to move to London for medical treatment where she lived with the Yeats family, thus finding herself surrounded by participants in the literary revival. After becoming co-editor of *The Irish Homestead*, she soon published poems in various publications before releasing her own collections in 1908.

GEORGE MOORE (1852–1933)

This Irish novelist, poet, critic, and short story author originally set out to pursue painting, studying in Paris where he befriended many of the leading French artists and writers. When he published *A Modern Lover* detailing the dalliances of a young man, the scandal caused his work to be removed from the two major libraries. His writing is often seen as influential to James Joyce and he is regarded as the first great modern Irish novelist.

SEAN O'CASEY (1880–1964)

A starkly committed Irish republican and socialist, he was the first Irish playwright of notoriety to utilize the Dublin working classes as subject matter.

DANIEL O'CONNELL (1775–1847)

Also known as The Liberator, he was a leader in Irish politics in the first half of the 19th century. As he was one of the leading campaigners for Catholic Emancipation, in 1823 he organized the Catholic Association, which played an important role in the passage of the Catholic Emancipation Act in 1829.

SEAN O'FAOLAIN (1900–1991)

O' Faolain charted the development of modern Ireland via the writing of ninety stories over the course of sixty years. Serving as director of the Arts Council of Ireland twice, he founded the Irish literary periodical *The Bell*.

CHARLES STEWART PARNELL (1846–1891)

With the noble title 'uncrowned King of Ireland', he is remembered as an advocate of freedom, and as a victim of the British Government and Catholic Church. He founded the Irish Parliamentary Party.

POOR RABBIN'S OLLMINIC

It is believed that Robert Herrick was the originator of this series that was published from the mid-1600s to early 19th century. The collection was one of satire and parody after which Benjamin Franklin's *Poor Richard's Almanac* was modeled.

SIR BOYLE ROCHE (1736–1807)

He was in open opposition to Catholic emancipation and a key player in Irish history. His speeches mirrored his support of the Act of Union with Britain. However, the language of his speeches was often unintentionally and comically laced with malapropisms.

COLONEL SAUNDERSON, MP (1837–1906)

An Irish politician, he was Justice of the Peace and Deputy Lieutenant for Cavan. His character was marked as being sternly religious and extremely sincere.

SARAH PURSER (1848–1943)

Studying first at the Dublin School of Art and then in Paris at the Academie Julian she worked primarily as a portraitist. She became wealthy through many commissions by wealthy clientele and through very wise investments.

GEORGE BERNARD SHAW (1856–1950)

Gaining his first writing profits from music and literary criticism, his talent was reserved for drama, evidenced by the sixty plus plays he authored. Marriage, class difference, and government led the list of social problems with which his plays, infused with necessary bits of comedy, dealt. Though this native Dubliner was awarded the coveted Nobel Prize for Literature, he accepted the honor but refused the money.

RICHARD BRINSLEY SHERIDAN (1751 - 1816)

His plays form an important link in the history of the comedy of manners in Ireland between the end of the 17th century and Oscar Wilde in the 19th. Not only an accomplished writer whose plays were performed at Covent Garden, he was a strong critic who supported the resistance of the colonists and gained a reputation as one of Britain's best orators.

DEAN JONATHAN SWIFT (1667–1745)

Remembered for works such as *Gulliver's Travels* and *A Modest Proposal*, this Anglo-Irish satirist, essayist, political pamphleteer, poet, and cleric eventually became Dean of St. Patrick's, Dublin. He published many works under pseudonyms or anonymously, but is mainly known for being one of the foremost satirists.

JUDGE NORBURY (JOHN TOLER) (1745–1831)

Born in County Tipperary, his witty sarcasm and dark humor hid his lack of legal skills in the courtroom. Thus, his courtrooms gained the reputation of being rather theatrical. Through less than legitimate means, he eventually reached the Bench and his reputation devolved to that of a corrupt and fearsome judge.

OSCAR WILDE (1854–1900)

Born in Dublin, he later moved to London and was a prominent society figure. Having written everything from children's stories, short stories, essays, several plays, and one novel, he became one of the most successful playwrights of the late Victorian era and was known for his depth of wit. A conviction of "gross indecency" with other men resulted in his imprisonment later in life, leading to his eventual professional downfall.

JOHN BUTLER YEATS (1839–1922)

This Irish artist was the father of William Butler and Jack Butler Yeats. His portrait of a young William is likely his best known painting.

WILLIAM BUTLER YEATS (1865–1939)

One of the most prominent figures in 20th century literature, he was a prime component behind the Irish Literary Revival. Being awarded a Nobel Prize in Literature for his poetry, he was the first Irishman to receive such an honor. Ironically, his works illustrating his opposition of the Nationalist movement completed after the receipt of the Prize are considered his greatest works..